1995

Harnessing Technology for Inclusive Governance

A Blueprint for Modernizing Public Participation

Mark K. Young

ACKNOWLEDGMENTS

There are several people whom I wish to thank. First, I would like to thank those who served on my Masters Research Project Committee: Dr. Howard H. Foster, Jr. and Dr. Rolf Pendall, professors with the Department of Community Planning and Area Development (CPAD) at the University of Rhode Island; and Marilyn Nicholls planner with the Planning and Zoning Department, Town of Greenwich, CT.

Next, I would like to thank those who work for the land preservation organizations profiled in this study who granted interviews and provided me with invaluable insights, including: Ms. Dawn Darbey-Dugan, with the Nantucket Land Bank; Mr. James Lengyel, with the Martha's Vineyard Land Bank; Mr. Stetson Eddy, with the Little Compton Agricultural Conservancy Trust; and Ms. Heidi Tarbox, with the Block Island Land Trust.

I would also like to thank my parents John and Mary Young who inspired me to write on the topic of open space preservation, and who continue to work to preserve open space in their community Greenwich, Connecticut. I hope this study can make a contribution to their cause and those shared by other communities.

Finally, I would like to thank George Elam for his patience and emotional support provided during the research process. His many selfless acts included allowing me to transform our Nantucket vacation into an opportunity to do the initial field research for this study.

TABLE OF CONTENTS

Page

LIST OF TABLES

Table | Page

LIST OF MAPS

Map | Page

CHAPTER ONE

INTRODUCTION

Problem Statement

Development pressures existing in the United States today have been responsible for the substantial disappearance of formerly available open space[1]. The general public perception is that the landscape/view is changing and that the change is not necessarily good. The loss of open land has brought public pressure on policy makers to decide the best use of remaining open space. Should it be left to developers to make the determination or should a community assert its own self-determined vision guided by professional expertise?

In 1853, Peter Schermerhorn wrote "that government existed only to protect private property" (Rosenzweig and Blackmar 1992: 50). While few today would debate the legitimacy of government at every level having a distinctly broader mandate; it is certainly true that the debate continues between would-be developers coping with myriad planning and zoning regulations and the government attempting to reach an equitable settlement among competing claims.

---

1 The definition of open space used herein is taken from the Connecticut General Statutes which provide a comprehensive description:

> Any area of land, including but not limited to forest land, tidal and inland wetlands and farm land, the preservation or restriction of the use of which would (1) maintain and enhance the conservation of natural or scenic resources, (2) protect natural streams or water supply, (3) promote conservation of soils, wetlands, beaches or tidal marshes, (4) enhance the value to the public of abutting or neighboring parks, forests, wildlife preserves, nature reservations or sanctuaries or other open spaces, (5) enhance public recreation opportunities, (6) preserve historic sites or (7) promote orderly urban or suburban development (1971: Sec. 12-107b [c]).

What a developer might view as confiscatory government intervention, a municipal wetlands agency could see as sound environmental restrictions for the greater public benefit. Operating within a framework that privately-held land subject to a degree of zoning regulation is a cornerstone of the American system, many communities have decided to adopt a pro-active stance rather than reactive when considering the future face of their communities.

Appreciation of the value of open space is not a new phenomenon. As early as 1850, New York City aldermen urged their city to acquire Jones Wood as a public park on three grounds: "Utilitarian claims that it would promote the city's commercial and physical health; social and moral arguments that it would 'improve' the 'disorderly' classes and foster order among them; and cultural contentions that it would display the cultivation of the leading citizens" (Rosenzweig and Blackmar 1992: 23). Frederick Law Olmsted and Calvert Vaux who together designed New York City's Central Park envisioned it "as a pastoral retreat from the pressures and aesthetic monotony of a growing city" (Rosenzweig and Blackmar 1992: 3). Open space either in its natural state or as a carefully manicured park has played a major role in defining the character of America's communities.

Thanks to the conservation movement in America in the latter part of the twentieth century, new elements of the value of open space and its disappearance are being appreciated by government policy makers. Nowhere has this been more graphically seen than along the once open space shorelines of the Mississippi River where overbuilding on unstable riverbanks in flood zones has led to erosion, polluted run-off from farm operations and then substantial loss of property in the 1993 flood. Recovery operations have even included the government buying some of the most vulnerable properties with tax payer money. As a result of the 1955 flash floods in Norwalk, CT, city officials directed rebuilding away from the riverbanks (thus creating riverside open space) and instituted minimum ground floor levels thereby qualifying property owners to participate in the National Flood Insurance Program. The governmental policy of preventive measures is generally seen as an enlightened move and a reasonable action to take in citizen and property protection. The seemingly incidental benefits of waterside open space greenways/walkways are an additional benefit to the public. Not overlooked are the benefits to marine life which is enhanced in the less-polluted environment.

While federal national disaster programs play a role in enabling communities to rebuild after an earthquake, hurricane or flood, they are not without cost. Aside from immediate emergency relief, the federal government at the state's request will offer to the affected property owner low-interest loans for cleanup and rebuilding. Tax payers across the board fund this government benevolence just as do private insurance rate payers when their insurance company is hit by an unprecedented number of claims for disaster relief. Although natural disasters will in the future recur, minimizing the likelihood of their consequent property and personal damage through sensible building and zoning regulations plus occasional land purchase (thus saving expenditure of disaster relief money) might seem to most people a sensible and appropriate government role.

Contrarily, when government intervenes to declare some undeveloped parcels off-limits because of a snail darter or a colony of owls, the public often becomes disenchanted. Simply because there is not yet a consensus on the public responsibility for endangered animal species, the public sees such intervention as reflecting woeful disregard for their jobs and property which may be within the affected boundary. As with every other government action, policy makers must steer a fine line in order to not appear to be acting in arbitrary fashion, or else risk loss of their position through the political process.

A piecemeal open space protection program, often characterized by unsolicited gift or response to a particular constituency, can give rise to inefficient development patterns in a community. Some open space properties by their very location may be virtually inaccessible to a large group of citizens and then of little general public benefit. Inefficient development patterns can significantly raise the cost of municipal service to tax payers. The cost to the public of sewer and water lines, roads, fire and police protection escalates when residential development is allowed all over the municipal landscape instead of planning for residential use in one sector and promoting open space use requiring few city services in another sector.

While acknowledging that municipal open space has obvious benefits to a community, some professionals in the land use field have expressed frustration with traditional methods for managing growth and retaining open space. Since the turn of the century, general plans, subdivision controls, zoning ordinances and building codes have been the traditional tools for guiding physical growth in American cities (Deakin 1989: 4). These tools have been criticized for lacking flexibility (Haar 1989; Stokes and others 1989). Lack of flexibility should not be confused with not having recourse to the appeals process. Adverse zoning decisions can be referred to municipal Boards of Appeals and then through the court system. Sometimes a higher board or court will render a more accommodating decision, sometimes not. Regulations by their very nature are restrictive. If deemed sufficiently restrictive, a court may decide they "amount to a taking of the land for which compensation must be paid by the public" (Reilly, ed. 1973: 145). Is the public's interest, both immediate and long term, being well served? Do autocratic inflexible rulings appear more equitable than examination on a case by case basis? Some traditional tools have been cited for lacking in significant ability to shape growth, control its timing or deal with many of its impacts, particularly financial and environmental ones (Fishman 1975: 61; Cigler 1980: 444; Barrese 1983: 235; Deakin 1989: 4; Schnidman 1978: 538).

Significance of Study

As previously mentioned, local governments are adopting goals for acquiring open space. Obstacles have arisen however, when attempting to achieve these goals. Acquisition of targeted open space parcels usually requires large amounts of money to be expended by a community following a lengthy approval process.

Policy makers seeking improvement over the status quo might

search for new approaches to the above-cited problems. In the classical-rational solving process, this search would be interpreted as identifying policy alternatives[2]. Traditional and innovative approaches will be considered in this study with particular attention being given to municipal open space acquisition programs funded by local real estate transfer tax revenues.

<u>Objectives of the Study</u>

This study will:

1. Examine traditional means of municipal open space acquisition;
2. Present options for financing municipal open space acquisition;
3. Compare alternative approaches for municipal acquisition/ preservation of open space;
4. Offer case studies of municipal open space acquisition funded by real estate transfer tax revenues;
5. Identify policy issues for consideration in designing a municipal open space acquisition program funded by real estate transfer tax revenues; and
6. Draw conclusions about implementation of a municipal open space acquisition program funded by real estate transfer tax revenues.

---

2 The classical-rational problem solving process involves six steps:

1. Define the problem;
2. Determine evaluation criteria;
3. Identify alternative policies;
4. Evaluate alternative policies;
5. Select the preferred policy; and
6. Implement the preferred policy (Patton and Sawicki 1993: 3).

Methodology

Literature will be reviewed to discuss the importance of open space in a community. Additional literature will be reviewed to discuss programs and means available to municipalities to secure open space for their citizens. Case studies of municipal open space acquisition funded by a real estate tax will then be offered. The examples include: the Nantucket Land Bank; the Martha's Vineyard Land Bank, the Block Island Land Trust, and the Little Compton Agricultural Conservancy Trust. Nantucket and Martha's Vineyard are located in Massachusetts. Little Compton and Block Island are located in Rhode Island. The case studies explored use primary and secondary data. Primary data has been collected from interviews conducted with representatives from the four land bank programs under study. These are complemented by existing literature on the same programs. The operational experiences of these case studies are synthesized and necessary and ancillary components of a land bank are exposed. A fifth case study is also offered for review concerning a land bank proposal that was defeated in the town of Greenwich Connecticut. After identifying common and unique features of the case studies, critical issues are highlighted to facilitate other communities in designing similar land bank programs.

To facilitate policy makers in the decision-making process the purchase alternative (funded by a real estate transfer tax) is compared alongside other alternatives commonly used by local governments to acquire and/or purchase open space, including: zoning mechanisms [incentive zoning, planned unit of development

(PUD), cluster zoning, large-lot zoning, transfer of development rights (TDR)], municipal tax incentives, gift, foreclosure, condemnation, intergovernmental transfers, and purchase funded by: municipal general funds, bond issues, and sales tax revenues. Criteria for comparison include: public investment, as measured by how costly a proposal might be; political acceptability, as measured by how politically feasible a proposal might be; and potential for preservation, as measured by the degree of permanency each alternative offers. A matrix is developed to present the results of these comparisons. Based on the analysis of data, guidelines are offered to facilitate use of a municipal open space acquisition program funded by a real estate transfer tax in other communities.

Organization of the Study

The study is divided into five chapters. Chapter One provides an introduction to the research problem, significance of the study, objectives of the study, methodology employed to obtain stated goals, and organization of the study. Chapter Two presents alternative approaches for municipal acquisition and/or preservation of open space. Chapter Three describes four case studies of municipal open space acquisition funded by real estate transfer tax revenues and one aborted attempt to enact such a program. Chapter Four raises policy issues for consideration when designing a program for municipal open space acquisition funded by real estate transfer tax revenues. Chapter Five offers final remarks.

CHAPTER TWO

ALTERNATIVE APPROACHES to MUNICIPAL ACQUISITION and/or PRESERVATION of OPEN SPACE

This chapter examines and discusses alternative approaches for municipalities to acquire and/or preserve open space along with possible financial strategies to accomplish this aim, including: zoning mechanisms [incentive zoning, planned unit of development (PUD), cluster zoning, large-lot zoning, and transfer of development rights (TDR)], municipal tax incentives, gifts, foreclosure, condemnation, intergovernmental transfers, and purchase funded by: municipal general funds, bond issues, sales tax revenues, and real estate transfer tax revenues.

The alternatives presented herein are not an exhaustive list of means available to a municipality to acquire and/or preserve open space, but their great number represents the many variations now available from which policy makers may choose. There are, however, constraints put upon the decision-making process. In the public sector, decisions will be contingent upon how much a proposal will cost (public investment[1]), and the level of public approval predicted (political acceptability). For a municipality to attain the goal of preserving open space, consideration should also be given to the degree of permanency each alternative offers (potential for preservation).

---

1 Public investment specifically refers to the dollar cost payable by the public sector to acquire and/or preserve open space; so-called "direct costs". This criteria does not quantify the indirect costs related to municipal open space acquisition such as property maintenance nor costs associated with zoning that can produce indirect costs such as those associated with suburban sprawl.

A matrix is presented in Table 1 to demonstrate graphically the desirability quotient of each alternative in relation to the criteria used for comparison. Descriptions of the alternatives follow to provide explanation for the ratings given.

Table 1. Comparison of Alternative Approaches for Municipal Acquisition and/or Preservation of Open Space.

Alternatives:	Public Investment	Political Acceptability	Potential for Preservation
Zoning: Incentive zoning	Low	Moderate	Moderate
PUD	Low	Moderate	Moderate
Cluster zoning	Low	Low	High
Large-lot zoning	Low	Low	Moderate
TDR	Low	Low	High
Municipal Tax Incentives	Low	Moderate	Low
Gift	Low	High	High
Foreclosure	Low	Low	Moderate
Condemnation	High	Low	High
Intergovernmental Transfers	Low	High	Moderate
Purchase: (Funding Options) Municipal General Funds	High	Low	High
Bond issues: 1. General Obligation	Low	High	High
2. Revenue	Low	Low	High
Sales Tax Revenues	High	Moderate	High
Real Estate Transfer Tax Revenues	Low	Moderate	High

Note: *Low, Moderate, and High* are ratings given for the desirability quotient of each alternative in relation to the criteria used for comparison.

Zoning:

Incentive zoning

This tool involves a trade-off agreement between the local regulatory authorities and a developer, where a developer is induced to provide open space in return for receiving a density bonus or some other key variance to the imposition of the normal regulations for his/her project.

In terms of evaluating this alternative the political acceptability of incentive zoning is directly related to the degree of the public accessibility and enjoyment of the benefit being gained. Because incentive zoning involves a surrender of a degree of the public's ability to rely on protective zoning regulations, the benefits from the surrender must be very apparent. The best ways of insuring political acceptability is to select the appropriate location and to mandate its permanency as open space through deed-restrictive language. There is no dollar cost to the public by such an arrangement particularly when management/maintenance responsibilities are assigned to the developer.

An interesting case relative to incentive zoning demonstrating some potential pitfalls was demonstrated at Grace Plaza, New York City, in 1973. The zoning code allowed builders of new corporate offices an additional ten square feet of floor area for every square foot of public space plaza. Other than laying out the requisite number of square footage for the plaza, the architect failed to incorporate any features which might make it attractive to local office workers. Hence, 'undesirables' took over followed by institution of a security person and guard dog. The usefulness of the plaza to the general public seemed nil. Next, "...plans were developed by the plaza management to enclose the space and create a shopping arcade. The proposal attracted a public debate over the potential privatization of the publicness of the space" (Carr and others 1992: 180). Since this time, the City in 1975 adopted a zoning amendment with specific guidelines on making such plazas "amenable" to the public (Carr and others 1992: 180).

Planned unit of development (PUD)

This is an example of a discretionary mechanism where "some towns have established so-called floating zones, authorized in the text of the ordinance but not mapped until a specific development is proposed and approved" (Reilly, ed. 1973: 189).

Planned unit development (PUD) regulations while not universally accepted across the country allow for flexibility in design in accordance with the environmental constraints of the property. Proponents of the PUD concept say that strict adherence to present minimum zoning regulations can often lead to inferior developments not tailored to the site in question (Reilly, ed. 1973: 189). PUDs may also reduce the effects of sprawl occasioned by more conventional zoning. Public opponents to the idea voice their inherent distrust of developers proposing a PUD believing that existing zoning is their last refuge and vowing a fight against 'spot zoning' (Reilly, ed. 1973: 190-1).

In terms of evaluating this alternative if an environment can be created where there is informed dialogue among the affected parties,

PUDs could become the vehicle to preserving valuable open space in a community as well as providing new development and on both accounts enjoy greater political acceptability. This alternative requires no outlay of public dollars, but the permanency of its open space preservation is contingent upon the deed-restrictive language for the project in question.

Cluster zoning

Cluster zoning is the term used when a developer may build the same number of units as in a conventional subdivision, but the lot size requirements will diminish, with a greater than usual percentage of land being dedicated for open space (or money is paid by the developer for municipal purchase of open space elsewhere). Cluster zoning is often done within planned unit of developments (PUDs). In Greenwich, Connecticut cluster zones requiring a minimum of 40% of the acreage to remain undeveloped, are a recent introduction. They are viewed as a response to situations where large properties were being carved up into subdivisions in accordance with the underlying zone and thus contributing to an emerging landscape of residential sprawl.

In terms of evaluating this alternative, the political acceptability of the cluster concept is only moderate because frequently the open space being set aside is for the use of a local homeowners association only and thus not practically publicly accessible nor generally visible to the public at large. In terms of public cost, there is none, as no purchase is made. Guarantee of permanency of this now municipally-owned open space is high unless a zoning change is approved.

Reliance, however, on zoning set asides to obtain municipal open space leads to a very piecemeal open space picture and does not necessarily assure that the priority parcels of open space in a community will be obtained.

Some states have attempted to meet some of the complaints about zoning set asides by initiating programs where fees instead of property set-asides are paid by the developer. For instance, in 1990, Connecticut enacted P.A. 90-239, which permits municipalities to enact a fee-in-lieu ordinance as part of their open space plan. The fee may not exceed 10% of the value of the land before subdivision, must be payable into an account separate from the town's general revenues and must be used for open space acquisition for recreational, passive or agricultural purposes (Wolfe and Horan 1991: 1-3).

Large-lot zoning

Large-lot zoning is a planning tool allowing for low-density residential development. At a minimum, this type of zoning prohibits more than one unit per acre. At the other extreme is San Luis Obispo County, California where a 320-acre minimum is used to maintain grazing land (Toner 1978: 2). The principal benefit of this technique is that no government funding is required for its implementation. Therefore, small cities and rural towns with limited planning budgets can easily apply this technique (Brower and others 1984: 96). However, an unfortunate consequence of large-lot zoning has been its sprawling pattern across the countryside.

The political acceptability of large-lot zoning is generally low, not only because privately-held land rarely invites public access, but also because a diminished land supply often causes prices for viable building parcels to escalate thus leading to an exclusionary environment. Nonetheless, a number of communities defend large-lot zoning citing the cost from public funds for sewers and connections to the municipal water supply if more intensively developed. Permanency of preservation of open space in these large-lots is less guaranteed than that offered by cluster zoning because these large-lot properties are privately held.

Transfer of development rights (TDR)

TDR is another alternative available to policy makers for preserving open space. TDR involves the establishment of sending (development rights) zones and receiving (development rights) zones. TDR occurs when private land owners purchase development rights from landowners in a sending zone, and apply them to their own land in the receiving zone, thereby increasing their land's development potential. The land from which the development rights were sent enjoys a high degree of guaranteed preservation as the once existing development rights are extinguished. As TDR is a transaction between private parties, no public access is gained and no public expenditure is required.

TDR offers a solution to the problem inherent in traditional land use regulation, that of windfalls and wipeouts. A windfall is an increase in value of real estate other than that caused by the owner or by general inflation, whereas a wipeout is a decrease in value of real estate not caused by the owner or by general deflation

(Hagman and Miscynski, 1978). Zoning for example can create high land values in areas zoned for high density development, or it can severely reduce values by zoning for low density. TDR offers a form of compensable land use regulation. In a TDR program the windfall, which comes in the form of a density bonus to a developer in the receiving zone is recaptured and transferred to the "loser," a landowner in the sending zone, as compensation for purchase of development rights (Schnidman, 1978).

Because designing a TDR program is a multi-layered process (Schnidman 1978: 549; Costonis 1975: 94), some communities may find this process too cumbersome. Public support may erode during any portion of the design phase of a TDR program, and thus the political acceptability of the scheme is threatened. Debate will arise over questions including: establishment of the planning district (where TDR's are permitted), the decision on the nature and number of rights issued, how the rights will be allocated, how the rights will be issued and taxed, public retirement of excess development rights and means for issuance of additional rights, if needed. In particular, problems may arise from constituents in the receiving zone who argue against increased densities being made available and constituents in the sending zone who view the newly-imposed development restrictions as a 'taking' of property rights worthy of 'just compensation' if unable to sell their development rights (Roddewig and Inghram 1987: 14).

Municipal tax incentives

Tax incentives for open space preservation rely on preferential assessment or differential taxation of such property by a municipality. It is a system in which a property owner who owns more land than is required to build a house has his/her tax assessments reduced on his/her excess property. The philosophy is that property owners would thereby lose their economic incentive to subdivide and sell off portions of their land for development. Usually a tax assessor values a property on the basis of its current income-producing capacity only, rather than on its higher real market value. This system in fact rewards the open-space property owner for not developing his open land by assessing him at a lower tax rate. Differential taxation of farmland and forests has been widely used as one cost-free means of preserving what much of the public see as good land uses.

The political acceptance of preferential taxation is only moderate. While admitting that it is a no up-front-cost way to preserve existing open space, the public also sees it as a mechanism for the rich to maintain their status quo and not pay their equitable share into the municipal coffers. Public acceptance is also dubious because it realizes that preferential taxation may not be sufficient to deter the ultimate development of the property. It is not fooled into believing that preferential taxation will guarantee preservation in perpetuity.

A disadvantage of using a tax incentive program is that it does not secure permanent open space preservation. Land owners may choose to develop their land at any time. "Preferential farmland assessment laws in California and New Jersey provide for recapture of taxes under a deferral theory whereby the property owner is required to pay back to the taxing authority the taxes he avoided by having his land classified as agricultural" (Reilly, ed. 1973: 129).

Federal tax deductions often play an incentive role in attracting open space property gifts to local land trusts or other conservation organizations and offer permanent land protection. On the negative side, these parcels of land are usually scattered all over the landscape ranging from fractions of an acre to vast tracts. They are usually closed to free public access and when left in their natural state offer little public use. Obviously, some properties have greater aesthetic appeal which a discerning public can appreciate when viewed from a public thoroughfare. Other properties may offer the less visible benefits of serving as a groundwater discharge area or flood water buffer to a community. Despite the removal of the donated properties from the local real property tax rolls, most Americans seem to approve of the intent motivating this federal tax incentive program.

Gifts

A gift of open space property to a municipality may be an outright donation with no strings attached. A beneficent property owner could deed an ideally situated acreage to his/her town requiring no "improvements" and without stipulation as to its future use. However, it is far more likely that the donor will place restrictions on his/her gift. In the deed of transfer, the donor may stipulate that the property is only to be used for passive recreational purposes under penalty of it reverting back to him/herself or estate. No public investment is required and the political acceptance is generally great for 'free' gifts of land in a desired location. The question of permanent preservation of open space will be dependent upon the restrictive covenants of the gift.

Situations may arise when a property owner is seeking to 'unload' a property for his/her own tax reasons without regard to any perceived public desire or need. Said property may be undevelopable with environmental problems rendering it inappropriate for even park use. Additionally, the property may have contaminants in its soil and trash calling for removal. Clearly, in this worst case scenario, a town is being offered little more than a liability. If however, the location of the property should meet either present or future open space needs, a town will knowingly assume the costs of repairing the property. If not, a town should decline the offer.

A municipality cannot rely on gifts alone when planning for orderly development. Political accountability should in fact dictate saying no to gifts of questionable value and accepting the inevitable that targeted acquisition of particular properties is the only sensible approach to sound community development. At the very least, if a donor insists on placing restrictions on his gift, the receiving town should seek to have the restrictions expire after a period of 20 years.

Foreclosure

There are so-called municipal land acquisition opportunities which can occur when a property owner defaults on his/her property tax. When it becomes clear usually after a period of many years that the municipality is unlikely to ever be able to collect the back taxes, the property title reverts to the town after appropriate legal proceedings. Occasionally, this may yield new park land or open space to the town. Often, the town will seek to sell the property on the open market with the monies going into the General Fund.

Assuming the town decides to dedicate the parcel for open space purposes, the permanency protection of the land is high and no public investment is required. However, the political acceptability is low because foreclosure situations are a distressing means for a municipality to meet its open space needs.

Condemnation

Targeted acquisition through condemnation is one approach available to municipalities. Basically, this municipal power, derived from the state confers the right to 'take' land for public purpose such as reservoir, highway and park development with the landowners receiving reasonable compensation. This exercise of 'police power' is one of the least popularly-appreciated powers held by the government. The public cost can be high, but the political acceptability is low. The permanency of protection factor may be termed high subject to varying political forces.

One illustration of just how contentious is this power is furnished in the history of New York's Central Park: "Municipal use of the power of eminent domain to take possession of more than eight-hundred acres of land for Central Park represented an unprecedented intervention in the real estate market" (Rosenzweig and Blackmar 1992: 7). In 1853, New York State Senator James Beekman wrote, "A park is not of sufficient public necessity to justify its being taken by the State in opposition to the wishes of the owners by the violent exercise of eminent domain" (Rosenzweig and Blackmar 1992: 59).

Many agreed with the Senator then as they might now. Is there a greater legitimacy for public health reasons in provision of parks than the undermining of private property holdings? While a park might in name promise access to all, would not in fact its benefits be utilized by the few in its immediate vicinity (Rosenzweig and Blackmar 1992: 59-91) ?

The political fallout of 'takings' is fraught with hazards. As neighborhoods are carved up, families uprooted, viewscapes changed in the name of progress, the public feels disenfranchised. In the case of the formation of New York City's Central Park, some lot owners within the proposed park borders and adjacent land owners fronting the park clearly stood to make a substantial profit by the government intervention in the private land market. Nonetheless, while squatters and small rentpayers were evicted from the park confines, and the tax payers were asked to bear the $5 million cost for compensating the landowners, the landowners still felt that they were being ill-treated. Adjacent land-owners to their great dismay were additionally required to pay 'benefit assessments' (Rosenzweig and Blackmar 1992: 81-82).

Future historians may or may not praise the urban vision underpinning the condemnation action, but the actual social cost to the fabric of an existing community is virtually incalculable. The opportunity for graft in the boundary-determining process and assessment valuations or the suspicion of same is so great, that the attempt to be fair and equitable rarely meets with public satisfaction.

Intergovernmental transfers

There exist cases when the state or federal government, or an agency thereof, may determine at the request of a municipality to either lease or sell at nominal price a property lying within the territorial limits of the municipality. The public cost is extremely low, therefore the political acceptability usually high, but the permanency issue is very questionable.

An instance of when public acceptability can become more tenuous occurred recently in Greenwich, Connecticut. The CT Department of Transportation sold to the town for $1.00 the Cos Cob power plant site and pond. The state stipulated however, that one half of the Power Plant site must be developed for moderate or affordable income housing, with the remaining acreage envisaged as a public-access waterfront park. Thus, the state achieved two desirable goals. In selling the power plant site and adjacent pond at an absurdly token price per parcel, one might read extreme generosity and public delight. And, in requiring construction of low income housing, the state showed enlightened social and economic awareness, facts guaranteed to please at least some voters.

Offsetting this munificent 'gift' is the fact that the state has shifted to the town responsibility for a site with an unknown quantity of toxic elements in the soil bordering an electric generating station where the neighbors worry about electro-magnetic field exposure. Do the benefits outweigh the liabilities? The issue continues to be debated town-wide. Local detractors to the scheme decry the state for dictating such terms while quietly acknowledging that they are not offering an alternate site for the required housing.

In another instance, the state of Connecticut recently in 1995 agreed to lease to Greenwich several acres bordering the waterfront which the town had sought for a marina and accessory parking under the CT Turnpike. On the short term, this appears to be a win-win situation. However, the town will invest an as-yet unknown sum of money to develop the marina. Because it remains state-owned land, the marina, in contrast to other town waterfront facilities which are restricted for town resident use only, will be open to the public at large. The fear is that adjacent residential streets will be clogged with out-of-town traffic. To be remembered is the fact that the state may eventually reclaim its land for other use. Here again is a situation where a town appears to be exercising fiscal prudence but in so doing is possibly abrogating its ability to freely select its land holdings and determine their best use. Just as gifts, intergovernmental transfers may have hidden costs.

Purchase

Purchase of land is yet another alternative available for a municipality to preserve and/or acquire open space. Both a fee-simple interest and less than fee-simple interest in land may be purchased. Using either option, open space can be preserved. Fee-simple acquisition, however, can offer the additional benefit of public access to land.

PDR or purchase for less than fee-simple interest is a technique used for acquisition of development rights to land or the right to determine that the land will not be developed. A development right is equal to the unused development potential permitted for a portion of land. Using PDR, land does not become publicly owned (or publicly accessible), rather a municipality acquires the development rights to land and then usually extinguishes them. PDR permits purchase by government of the development rights to land under voluntary agreements with landowners in consideration for deed-restricting future development of the land (Daniels 1991: 421).

The price of development rights is usually determined by the difference between the value of the highest and best-use of the land and the current undeveloped use (Thompson 1984: 66). In theory, the purchase of development rights would be substantially less expensive than the purchase of land in fee-simple. In practice though, public acquisition of development rights can cost over fifty percent of fair market value and cost may exceed the value of land as open space (Daniels 1991: 423). Like fee-simple acquisition, the funds required may overwhelm a town's budget.

Open space purchase by its very nature requires an outlay of municipal funds even when the price may be negotiated to a less-than-market cost. Resources available to fund municipal acquisition of open space include: municipal general funds, bond issues, sales tax revenues, and real estate transfer taxes.

Municipal general funds

Funds for purchase of open space can be found in a municipality's operating budget. Rarely, however, are funds dedicated for this purpose. Therefore a budget request to fund an open space acquisition initiative must compete with other numerous requests, not all of which can be granted by a constrained municipal operating budget.

Because the public cost may be high when borne only by the municipal general funds, political acceptability of the proposition will be almost wholly contingent upon the location of the property and the public consensus as to its value for their enjoyment. It should be noted, however, that the present climate of citizen concern over rising municipal costs, escalating land prices, and worry about property tax assessments does not point to a rosy future for municipal open space purchases. But, when it happens, the benefit is that uncertainty about the immediate fate of the open space is eliminated, but only to the extent that the town resolution enabling the purchase carries language explicitly saying that the purchase is for open space or park purposes. Otherwise, other municipal land use proponents will vie for the land. The Connecticut General Statutes offer a solution to this problem through Sec. 7-131n which mandates that a municipality provide comparable replacement land if it takes land which was previously intended for open space purposes.

Bond issues

General obligation (GO) bonds

Municipal governments usually rely on property taxes and collection of fees to subsidize service and capital expenditures. Occasionally, they are in a position to draw upon reserves. In instances when such reserves do not exist and general funds are otherwise earmarked, a town may decide to issue General Obligation bonds to fund a particular need such as land acquisition rather than raise taxes substantially, an obvious political liability. The theory is that the long-term public benefit of such "improvements" will outweigh the long-term small tax increase. General Obligation bonds are backed by the full faith and credit of the issuing municipality. Where the town is considered to be financially strong, the bondholders are secure in the promise of repayment. From an investor's point of view, municipal bonds usually offer the advantage of federal tax-free income, thus their political acceptability may be rated high, and their public investment small.

Revenue bonds

In contrast, Revenue Bonds which are secured by anticipated revenues from an activity such as a sports arena are considered more risky and therefore enjoy less public acceptance. The permanency of protection of acquired land does not change whether the purchase is funded outright or through bond issues. The guarantee for preservation of open space is high unless or until a municipality deems it no longer to be in the public interest to do so. Again, deed-restricting the land can prevent municipally acquired open space reverting into developable land.

Despite the attractive elements of both types of bonds some fiscally conservative municipalities such as Greenwich, Connecticut pride themselves on their 'pay-as-you-go' policy and have for the past twenty-five years refused to consider this method of financing land purchases.

Clearly, there are pros and cons to the bonding approach. Prudent planning and saving for future municipal needs may only rarely accommodate the expensive acquisition of a property which unexpectedly comes on the market. Other competing municipal needs may dictate the town passing up the brief window of opportunity to acquire a choice piece of land which auxiliary funds from bonding might accommodate. Yet, a fiscally prudent town can always cite instances in other towns of fiscal improvidence.

Sales tax revenues

Some states permit municipalities to impose their own sales tax, the revenues to be used for local purposes such as infrastructure improvements or other municipal purposes. In 1934, New Mexico first imposed a gross receipts tax, the constitutionality of which was upheld by the New Mexico Supreme Court in 1938. Thanks in part to citizen lobbying efforts both in the 1980's and 1990's in Albuquerque, referenda were passed permitting allocation of a portion of the gross receipts monies to acquisition of open space during two three-year periods. Having a defined period of time for the sales tax certainly improved its political acceptability. In a rather novel arrangement, the city purchased a vast 7000+ acre tract of forest land on the side of a nearby mountain which it exchanged with the U.S. Forest Service for some 17,000 acres elsewhere in Albuquerque and across New Mexico. The net result is that precious vistas have been saved for Albuquerque citizens to enjoy. As well, the potential of future earnings on the other lands to be sold is clearly construed as a benefit of the program. While there is substantial initial public investment, the political acceptability is reported to be high in this case namely because the acquired land is deemed to be of high visual value, and there is the promise of eventual returns on their investment when some of the 17,000 acres are sold (Hart 1995).

Nonetheless, the visible success of this undertaking has its down side. Citizen groups espousing other causes such as public safety and more police are seeking their opportunity to have a share of the gross receipts tax pie, and open space acquisition proponents will have to wage an even harder battle next time against competing interest groups (Hart 1995). It is also true that a sales tax has a greater negative impact on the less affluent as that they are called upon to pay proportionately more than the well to do and may in fact choose to shop in neighboring towns and avoid the sales tax.

Real estate transfer tax revenues

Some states have granted to specific municipalities or counties the power to impose a local real estate transfer tax, the funds of which to be used to acquire open space or the development rights thereto.

In four instances which will be discussed in greater detail in the next chapter, the transfer tax tool was given to empower municipalities to provide public access to beaches, shorelines, woods and moors that were rapidly disappearing from the landscape as new home-owners asserted their exclusive property rights. Regulatory powers and appeals for scarce state funds were proving inadequate to address the problem.

As land is purchased by a municipality using revenues from the transfer tax, remaining open space properties escalate in value. Countering claims that this tool simply acts as an aid to wealthy land owners, proponents of the plans respond by saying that the open space properties permit access and enjoyment by a vast spectrum of the public in addition to providing a recreational resource and at no cost to the public at large. The property owners and tax payers affirming their approval of this approach to open space preservation for their communities realize that the properties will be removed from the tax rolls, and as a result they will be relieved from bearing future municipal costs with the land remaining in undeveloped state.

Municipal open space acquisition funded by a real estate transfer tax as one approach compares favorably with the more commonly used approach of municipal open space acquisition funded by a municipal general funds. While both mechanisms may achieve an identical result, they differ in their approaches. Administrators of a municipal open space acquisition program funded by real estate transfer tax revenues typically chart a map of desired parcels. When they become available, the program administrators especially if they have bonding powers, possess the financial means to readily secure the property or the development rights thereto. While program administrators are elected for terms ranging up to five years, accountability for their actions at the election booth is generally of a non-political nature.

However, a contrary example is noteworthy in an instance of outright municipal acquisition. In a study of Fairfield, Connecticut entitled The Politics of Privilege, author Donald Greenberg cites former First Selectman, John Sullivan. "Sullivan's basic position was to express no position on any zoning matter which did not directly affect the whole town...but, over the years a neighborhood that was directly affected by an adverse zoning decision would often find itself a recipient of land set aside under the Open Space Program" (Greenberg 1994: 75). This case is not to disparage municipal compensatory action, but rather is to illustrate that opportunities exist in municipal government where influence in the right places can favor one constituency above consideration of the overall master plan for open space needs. From the public perspective, a declared land bank for open space preservation is presumed to be as it is named. A municipality acquiring land without explicit limited purpose arouses public concern as to its future disposition and invites heated competition to its proper use.

The ability to act swiftly with flexibility is essential to any preservation program. Although a municipality can on occasion decide to take an option on a particular property thus permitting time for the review/approval process, it is unlikely that the tax payers will endorse such activity on a frequently repeated basis and see their tax bills rise as a consequence. A municipal open space acquisition program funded by real estate transfer tax revenues is a vigorous and far-sighted plan offering public policy makers the tools to act decisively to protect natural and undeveloped areas, both small and large, for ecological, scenic or recreational purposes.

Lastly, it must be stressed that while fee-simple acquisition funded by municipal general funds and real estate transfer tax-funded acquisition both enable the purchase of property, there is still the question of property maintenance. Municipalities in the mid-1990's are heeding tax payer calls for reduced government spending and downsizing. Often parks personnel are the first to be eliminated. Where some properties clearly require more maintenance than others, the real estate transfer tax-funded programs are in a better financial position than the average municipal operating budget to provide the needed management.

Diminished government spending often translates to open space acquisition being relegated to the end of the list behind other more obvious needs such as infrastructure repair or state-mandated programs. Thus, in frequency of occurrence, municipalities without real estate transfer tax-funded programs lag well behind municipalities with such programs in utilizing the fee-simple acquisition technique to increase their open space inventory.

Compared to other alternatives commonly chosen by local policy makers to preserve open space, a municipal open space acquisition program funded by real estate transfer tax revenues: requires no public outlay of funds, may be more politically palatable than traditional means of land acquisition because it is not supported by general revenues, and offers guaranteed preservation of open space as well as affording the opportunity to provide public access to land.

CHAPTER THREE

CASE STUDIES

In this chapter, profiles of four municipal open space acquisition programs funded by real estate transfer tax revenues are presented. The programs are operating in Nantucket and Martha's Vineyard in Massachusetts; and Little Compton and Block Island (New Shoreham) in Rhode Island. Also provided is a brief discussion of a (defeated) proposal for Greenwich, Connecticut. The four active programs do not purport to be a complete listing of existing municipal open space acquisition programs funded by a real estate transfer tax, rather it is their close proximity to one another, and to this writer a Connecticut resident that justified their selection for study.

Each active program profile includes: location orientation, program origin, program purposes, program administration, powers of program administrators, transfer tax imposed and descriptive data on land acquired. Because Nantucket was the first town to establish a municipal open space acquisition program funded by a real estate transfer tax, added historical background is provided in this profile. More information on the four active programs is provided in the state enabling legislation required to establish each program[3].

---

3 State enabling legislation empowering each community to establish a municipal open space acquisition program funded by a real estate transfer tax, as well as model legislation drafted by the Massachusetts Audubon Society for establishing such a program, is reprinted in the Appendix.

1. Nantucket, Massachusetts

Location orientation

Nantucket is a 50-square-mile island located 22 miles south of Cape Cod. It is both a town and county of Massachusetts. Since 1990, the number of year round residents has climbed 13% and is now estimated to be 6,794 in 1995. There are 7,102 dwelling units on the island. The population increases dramatically during the summer months to some 40,000 persons, a figure which reflects day tourists, week visitors, summer help, and vacation home residents, according to the Nantucket Planning Department (1995). Tourism and construction provide the financial base of the island's economy.

Program origin

For years, residents have sought to preserve Nantucket's special qualities by controlling the pace and character of local development. The island administers some of the nation's oldest and most rigorous architectural controls, contains one of the earliest designated historic districts and has one of the most active and effective conservation organizations in the United States with land holdings across the island. However, by 1982, islanders had only one and a half of the eighty miles of shoreline to call their own (Stolz 1990: 25). Combined with a development boom in the early 1980's, this fact prompted local officials to pursue a means to preserve strategic parcels of undeveloped land ideally located between existing open space parcels. Following a growth management conference, a document entitled "Goals and Objectives for Balanced Growth" was written in 1983, in which Goal A was to "establish...an island wide open space system." The path to this goal was supplied by Nantucket town planner, William Klein, who was inspired that the solution to problems of rampant growth might lie in devising some way to tie conservation efforts to development pressure. "I woke up one night and said, 'This is what we have to do: put two disparate ideas together. Hitch the conservation wagon to the wild runaway real estate market.' It was a natural" (Stolz 1990: 26).

On most real estate transactions, a percentage of the purchase price would be set aside to pay for open space acquisition. The idea was visionary. Nantucket Land Bank Director, Dawn Darbey-Dugan acknowledges, "What we are doing is for future generations, not ourselves...We need grander thinking. Basically, we should be protecting just about everything that is left. To think that there will always be property to develop or to conserve is just not far-sighted," (Stolz 1990: 26). In December 1983, the state legislature gave Nantucket the authority to establish its program and the Nantucket Land Bank Act was signed into law (Massachusetts Acts: Chapter 669). In February 1984, local approval was obtained at a special town meeting. Since then, it has served as a model for other communities.

Program purposes

The Nantucket Land Bank was established for the purpose of preserving: ocean, harbor and pond frontage in the form of beaches, dunes and adjoining backlands; barrier beaches; fresh and saltwater marshes, estuaries and adjoining uplands; heathland and moors; existing and future wellfields and aquifer recharge areas; and land

land used or to be used for agricultural purposes. Land acquired may also be used to provide: access to ocean, harbor and pond frontage; for bicycle paths; and for future public recreational facilities and use (Massachusetts Acts 1983: Chapter 669, Sec. 5).

Land is to be retained in its natural, scenic or open condition. The following activities are prohibited except upon approval by the Massachusetts Secretary of Environmental Affairs: building or road construction, dumping, removal of vegetation, excavation, dredging, or any other acts or uses detrimental to preserving the natural condition of the land (Massachusetts Acts 1983: Chapter 669, Sec. 6).

Program administration

The Nantucket Land Bank is managed by a commission consisting of five trustees, elected for staggered five year terms (Massachusetts Acts 1983: Chapter 669, Sec. 3). The stewardship and monitoring of Land Bank properties is the responsibility of the trustees.

Powers of program administrators

The Nantucket Land Bank commission has the authority to acquire and dispose of interests in land on Nantucket Island and the surrounding islands of Tuckernuck and Muskeget. The Land Bank is further authorized to receive voluntary contributions of money, grants or loans in funds. Land may be acquired by purchase, gift, or devise. On a case by case basis, subject to a town vote, the commission is also empowered to take land by eminent domain, incur debt and issue bonds pledging the full faith and credit of the town. Properties acquired by the Land Bank must be retained in their predominantly natural state and cannot be sold without a two-thirds roll call vote of the state legislature (Massachusetts Acts 1983: Chapter 669, Sec. 4).

Transfer tax

The 'bank' or fund of the Nantucket Land Bank receives a real estate transfer fee of 2% of the sales price paid by the purchaser. The revenue is placed in a revolving account which can be drawn upon to acquire property, staff support and professional services connected with the management of the land. The first $100,000 of the sale is exempt from the tax for first-time home buyers. Transfers made without consideration are also exempt (see Appendix for further exemptions). Payment is evidenced by stamping the deed of sale prior to official recording of the transaction (Massachusetts Acts, 1983: Chapter 669, Sec. 10, 12). New legislation would be required to repeal or amend the tax (Darbey-Dugan 1995).

Descriptive data

1,165 acres of land on Nantucket Island have been permanently preserved by the land bank as of April, 1995 (Darbey-Dugan 1995). This represents 3.69% of the island's 31,520 acres. Combined with land preserved by private conservation organizations, over one-third of the Island is now protected from development[4]. Land acquired is

---

[4] The contributions made by non-profit conservation organizations towards open space preservation in Nantucket are substantial. The following lists some of the organizations and the acres they are preserving on the Island and is evidence that the Land Bank program serves as a supplement to an already established land conservation movement:

1. The Nantucket Conservation Foundation-8,345 acres or 26.37%;
2. The Massachusetts Audubon-941 acres or 2.98%;
3. The Trustees of Reservations-921 acres or 2.92%;
4. The Sconset Trust, Inc.-62 acres or 0.1%;
5. The Nature Conservancy-18 acres or 0.05%.

held in fee-simple interest. Acquisitions are made in conformance with the open space plan drafted annually by the land bank commission. Map 1 shows land preserved by the land bank as of 1990. Special permission has been granted by program administrators to reprint this map.

MAP 1. Land Preserved by the Nantucket Land Bank

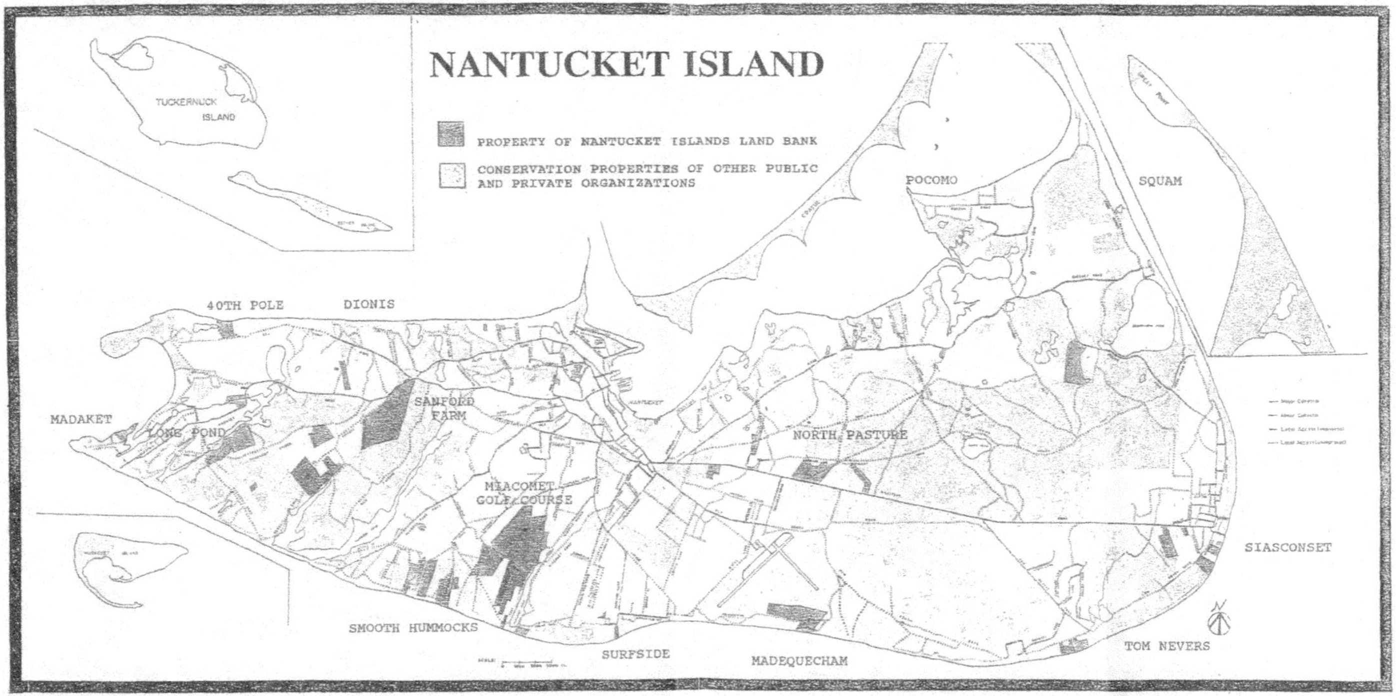

2. Martha's Vineyard, Massachusetts

Location orientation

Martha's Vineyard is the largest island in New England, with a total land area of about 100 square miles. It is located five miles south of Cape Cod, Massachusetts. Martha's Vineyard is part of Dukes County. Dukes County is composed of the island of Martha's Vineyard, the Elizabeth Islands and Norman's Land Island. There are seven towns in the county, six are located on Martha's Vineyard. The Martha's Vineyard Commission estimates the year-round population to be 13,000 residents increasing to 35,000 during the summer. This seasonal activity provides the primary financial base to the island's community.

Program origin

The design of the Martha's Vineyard Land Bank replicates that of Nantucket with some exceptions. Residents of Martha's Vineyard saw Nantucket successfully use real estate transfer tax revenues to fund municipal open space acquisition and they wanted to duplicate the process on their island. Martha's Vineyard Land Bank Executive Director James Lengyel reports, "Nantucket was the model for Martha's Vineyard. The feeling was, 'See, it works. It does the job. Nantucket is saving land," (Stolz 1990: 26).

Two years after the Nantucket Land Bank was established, the Martha's Vineyard program began. Legislation was enacted December 20, 1985 which gave the six towns on Martha's Vineyard authority to establish the Dukes County Land Bank, popularly known as the Martha's Vineyard Land Bank (Massachusetts Acts: Chapter

736). Local approval was obtained at a town meeting May 12, 1986. Any town that is a member of the land bank may withdraw therefrom upon a majority vote of the town's residents.

Program purposes

The list of lands to be preserved by the Martha's Vineyard Land Bank closely parallels that of the Nantucket Land Bank. Like Nantucket, the Martha's Vineyard Land Bank was established for the purpose of preserving: land to protect existing and future well fields, aquifers and recharge areas; agricultural lands; forest land; fresh and salt water marshes and other wetlands; ocean and pond frontage. beaches, dunes, and adjoining backlands, to protect their natural and scenic resources; land for nature and wildlife preserve; and land for passive recreational use. Distinct from Nantucket, this program's list of purposes also includes land to protect scenic vistas; and easements for trails (Massachusetts Acts 1985: Chapter 736, Sec. 5). Trails are a greater attraction on Martha's Vineyard compared to Nantucket because the island is larger and the vegetation is more dense.

Like Nantucket, land is to be retained in its natural, scenic or open condition. And like Nantucket, the same restrictions regarding alteration of the land apply except upon approval from the Massachusetts Secretary of Environmental Affairs (Massachusetts Acts 1985: Chapter 736, Sec. 6).

Program administration

The land bank is managed by a commission of seven persons, six of whom are residents from each town on Martha's Vineyard (Chilmark, Gay Head, Oak Bluffs, Tisbury and West Tisbury). The

Massachusetts Secretary of Environmental Affairs is also a voting member of the land bank commission. Following Nantucket's example, the other six members are elected to the commission and serve for staggered three-year terms (Massachusetts Acts 1985: Chapter 736, Sec. 3).

Powers of program administrators

The Martha's Vineyard Land Bank has the authority to acquire and dispose of interests in land on Martha's Vineyard. Their additional powers match those given to the Nantucket Land Bank Commission. Like the Nantucket example, certain powers are granted only on a case by case basis. Distinct from Nantucket, these powers can be employed only after not one, but six towns give their consent. (Massachusetts Acts 1985: Chapter 736, Sec. 4).

Transfer tax

The components of the transfer tax are identical to the Nantucket model. A 2% tax is imposed on the sale of real estate and is paid by the purchaser. Likewise, the first $100,000 of the total purchase price is exempt from the tax for first time home buyers The measure used to enforce the tax is also the same. In contrast to Nantucket, a two-thirds vote by the towns' electors is required to repeal or amend the tax (Massachusetts Acts 1985: Chapter 736, Sec. 10, 12).

Descriptive data

1,067 acres of land on Martha's Vineyard have been permanently preserved by the Martha's Vineyard Land Bank as of January 1, 1995. This is 1.7% of the island's 62,537 acres. Less than 100 acres are held in conservation easement, the remaining is held in fee-simple interest (Lengyel 1995). Acquisitions are made in conformance with the open space plan drafted annually by the land bank commission. Map 2 shows land preserved by the Martha's Vineyard Land Bank as of 1994. Special permission has been granted by program administrators to reprint this map.

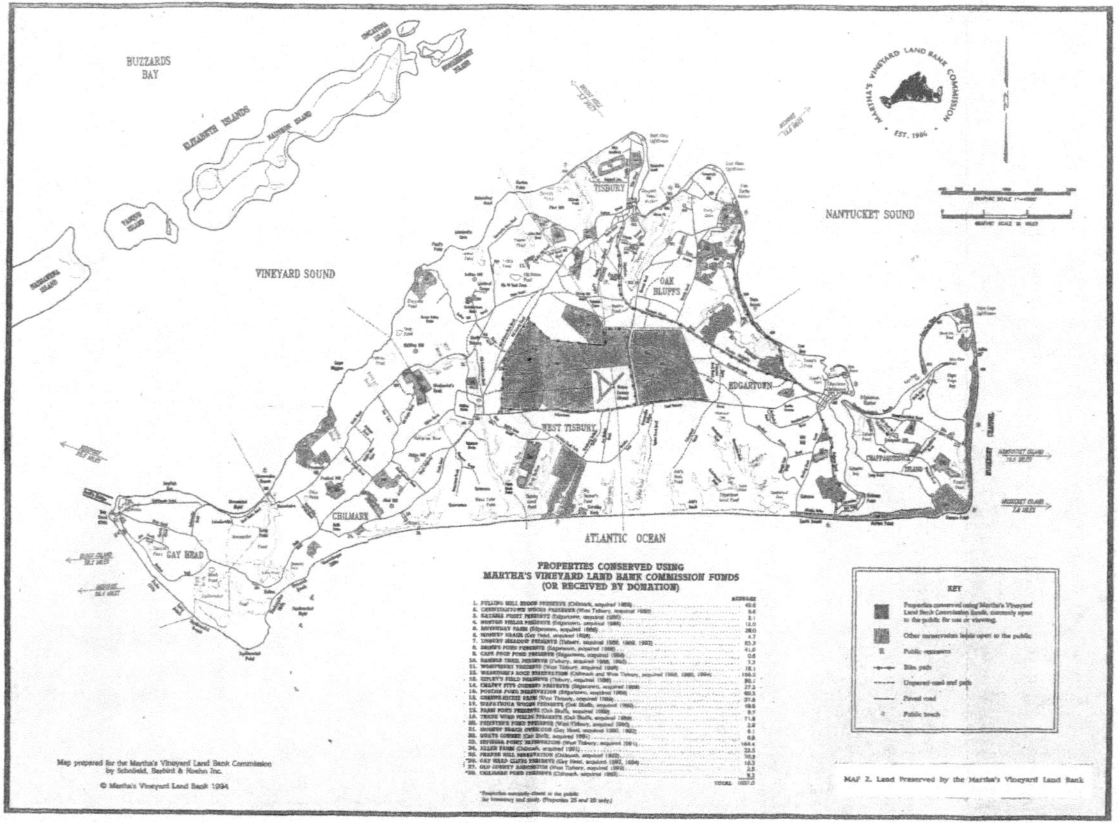

MAP 2. Land Preserved by the Martha's Vineyard Land Bank

3. Little Compton, Rhode Island

Little Compton is a coastal rural farming community located about thirty-two miles southeast of Providence and twelve miles south of Fall River, Massachusetts. It is bounded by Massachusetts on the east; by the Atlantic Ocean on the south; by the Sakonnet River on the west and by the town of Tiverton on the north. One of the six communities in Newport County, the town has a land area of 21.6 square miles. The 1990 U.S. Census reports the year round population to be 3,339. The Little Compton Planning Board estimates that the population doubles during the summer months (1995). Agriculture and seasonal business related to tourism are the most significant elements in the local economy.

Program origin

After Nantucket, and at the same time as Martha's Vineyard established its program, so, too, did Little Compton. "We're part of Nantucket's progeny," reports Stetson Eddy, Secretary of the Little Compton Agricultural Conservancy Trust, the official name of the municipal open space acquisition program funded by a real estate transfer tax (Stolz 1990: 26). The design of the program, however, varies somewhat from the Nantucket model.

The state legislature gave Little Compton authority to establish a land bank on May, 1985 (Rhode Island Public Laws: Chapter 16). Local approval was received at a Financial Town Meeting in May, 1986.

Program purposes

Distinct from the Nantucket and Martha's Vineyard programs, the

Little Compton Agricultural Conservancy Trust was established for the primary purpose of preserving farm land. Its secondary purposes includes preserving open space; fresh and saltwater marshes; estuaries and adjoining uplands; and groundwater recharging areas. Land acquired may also be used to provide public access to the ocean; for bicycle paths; and future public recreational facilities (Rhode Island Public Laws 1985: Chapter 16, Sec. 1).

With the exception of property acquired for public recreational use, land is to be used for open space or agricultural use (Rhode Island Public Laws 1985: Chapter 16, Sec. 5). Upon acquisition of property public use and enjoyment is permitted as long as it is consistent with the natural and scenic resources of the land (Rhode Island Public Laws 1985: Chapter 16, Sec. 6).

Program administration

The Little Compton Agricultural Conservancy Trust is managed by seven trustees who serve staggered terms for five years. The current chairpersons of the town conservation commission and the town planning board serve as trustees. The remaining five trustees are appointed by the town council, in contrast to Nantucket which requires members to be elected. Also in contrast, it is mandated that at least one trustee of the Little Compton Agricultural Conservancy Trust be an active farmer (Rhode Island Public Laws 1985: Chapter 16, Sec. 2).

Powers of program administrators

The Little Compton Agricultural Conservancy Trust administrators have the authority to acquire and dispose of interests in land in

Little Compton. Selling of land is permitted subject to a town vote (Eddy 1995). Like the Nantucket model, trustees are authorized to receive voluntary contributions of money, grants or loans; and land may be acquired by purchase, gift or by will (Rhode Island Public Laws 1985: Chapter 16, Sec. 5). In contrast to the Nantucket model, trustees may not incur debt, issue bonds or exercise the power of eminent domain.

Transfer tax

The components of the transfer tax are similar to the Nantucket model. Like Nantucket, the current tax rate is set at 2%, to be paid by the purchaser. However, the state enabling legislation permits the rate to be raised to 5%. The first $75,000 of the sales price is exempt for first time home buyers instead of the $100,000 permitted by Nantucket where real estate is more expensive. Like Martha's Vineyard, the electors of the town are empowered to repeal or amend the tax (Rhode Island Public Laws 1985: Chapter 16, Sec. 7-8).

Descriptive data

648 acres of land in Little Compton have been permanently preserved by the Little Compton Agricultural Conservancy Trust as of March 1995 (Eddy 1995). This represents 4.36% of the town's 14,848 acres. Nine acres are held in conservation easement, 469 in development rights and 170 acres are in fee simple interest (Eddy 1995). In accordance with the state enabling legislation, priority has been given to acquisition of development rights of agricultural lands (Rhode Island Public Laws 1985: Chapter 16, Sec. 5). Map 3 shows land preserved by the Little Compton Agricultural Conservancy

Trust as of 1994. Special permission has been granted by program administrators to reprint this map.

MAP 3. **Land Preserved by the Little Compton Agricultural Conservancy Trust.**

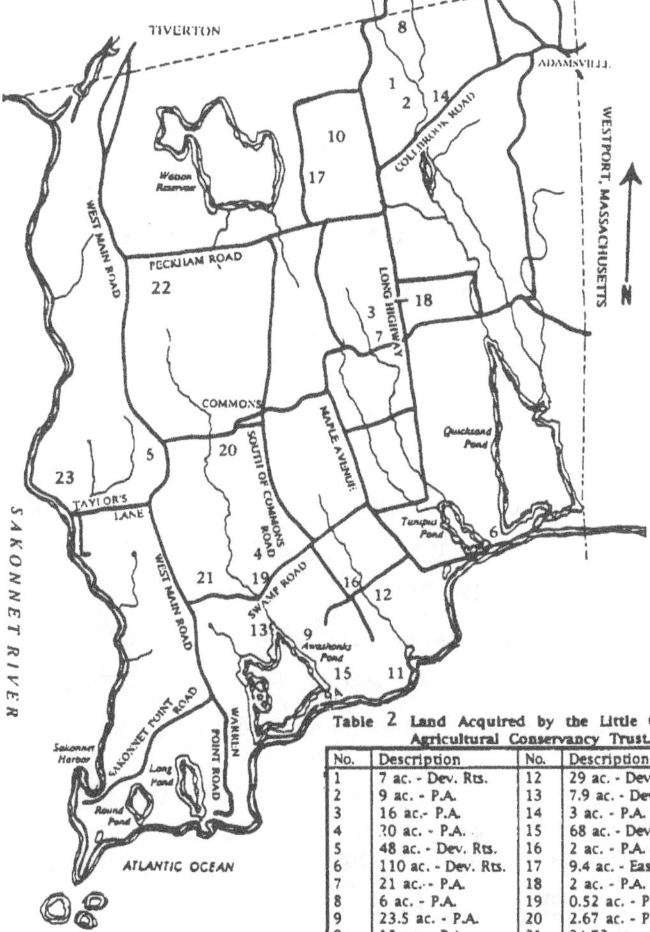

Table 2 Land Acquired by the Little Compton Agricultural Conservancy Trust.

No.	Description	No.	Description
1	7 ac. - Dev. Rts.	12	29 ac. - Dev. Rts.
2	9 ac. - P.A.	13	7.9 ac. - Dev. Rts.
3	16 ac.- P.A.	14	3 ac. - P.A.
4	20 ac. - P.A.	15	68 ac. - Dev. Rts.
5	48 ac. - Dev. Rts.	16	2 ac. - P.A.
6	110 ac. - Dev. Rts.	17	9.4 ac. - Easement
7	21 ac.- P.A.	18	2 ac. - P.A.
8	6 ac. - P.A.	19	0.52 ac. - P.A.
9	23.5 ac. - P.A.	20	2.67 ac. - P.A.
9a	15 ac. - P.A.	21	24.72 ac. - P.A.
10	5 ac. - Dev. Rts.	22	2 ac. - P.A.
11	2.7 ac. - P.A.	23	124 ac. - Dev. Rts.

Notes:
Dev. Rts. = Development Rights
P.A. = Public Access, fee interest
Source: Little Compton Agricultural Conservancy Trust

4. New Shoreham, (Block Island) Rhode Island

Location orientation

New Shoreham is located 12.5 miles south of the mainland. It is one of nine towns in Washington County, Rhode Island. The town is popularly referred to as Block Island. It has a land area of about ten-square miles. The local Chamber of Commerce estimates Block Island to be home to 800 year-round residents. Peak summer population is estimated at 13,000 persons. Seasonal business activity provides the financial base of the island's economy.

Program origin

Six months after the Little Compton Agricultural Conservancy Trust was established, Block Island became the second community in Rhode Island to establish a municipal open space acquisition program funded by real estate transfer tax revenues having received its state authorization in June 1986 (Rhode Island Public Laws 1986: Chapter 286). Local approval for the program was received at a special town meeting in October 1986. A staff member of the Block Island Land Trust, the official name of the program, reports, "Nantucket was the model used for establishing this program" (Tarbox 1995). The program's purposes and management are akin to the Nantucket model.

Program purposes

The language describing the purposes for the Nantucket Land Bank is repeated in the enabling legislation for the Block Island Land Trust. It refers to preserving open, agricultural, or littoral property, including: existing and future well fields, aquifers and recharge areas; fresh and salt water marshes and adjoining uplands; barrier beaches; wildlife habitats; land for bicycling and hiking paths and for future recreational use; and land for agricultural use (Rhode Island Public Laws 1986: Chapter 268, Sec. 1). Also found in this list is, "land to provide views of the ocean, harbors, and ponds." This parallels the language in the Martha's Vineyard legislation which lists "land to protect scenic vistas" (Massachusetts Acts 1985: Chapter 736, Sec. 5). Restrictions to land-altering activity are the same as those listed for the Little Compton Agricultural Conservancy Trust.

Program administration

The Block Island Land Trust is managed by five trustees who serve for staggered four-year terms. Like the Nantucket model, trustees are elected (Rhode Island Public Laws 1986: Chapter 268, Sec. 2).

Powers of program administrators

The Block Island Land Trust administrators have all the same powers granted to the trustees of the Little Compton Agricultural Conservancy Trust. In addition, trustees of the Block Island Land Trust are authorized, on a case by case basis, to incur debt and issue bonds pledging the full faith and credit of the town (Rhode Island Public Laws 1986: Chapter 268, Sec. 5, 12). But, like Little Compton, trustees of the Block Island Land Trust may not exercise the power of eminent domain.

Transfer tax

All of the elements of the Nantucket transfer tax are the same for the Block Island Land Trust except for the tax rate and the $75,000 exemption extended to first-time home buyers. This program is funded by a 3% tax on the total purchase price. The electors of the town are empowered to amend or repeal the tax (Rhode Island Public Laws 1986: Chapter 268. Sec. 6-7, 9).

Descriptive data

184 acres of land on Block Island have been permanently preserved by the Block Island Land Trust as of January 1, 1995 (Tarbox 1995). This represents 3.04% of the town's 6,030 acres. 117 acres are held in conservation easement. The remaining 67 acres are fee-simple interests. Map 4 shows land preserved by the Block Island Land Trust as of 1994. Special permission has been granted by program administrators to reprint this map.

MAP 4. Land Preserved by the Block Island Land Trust

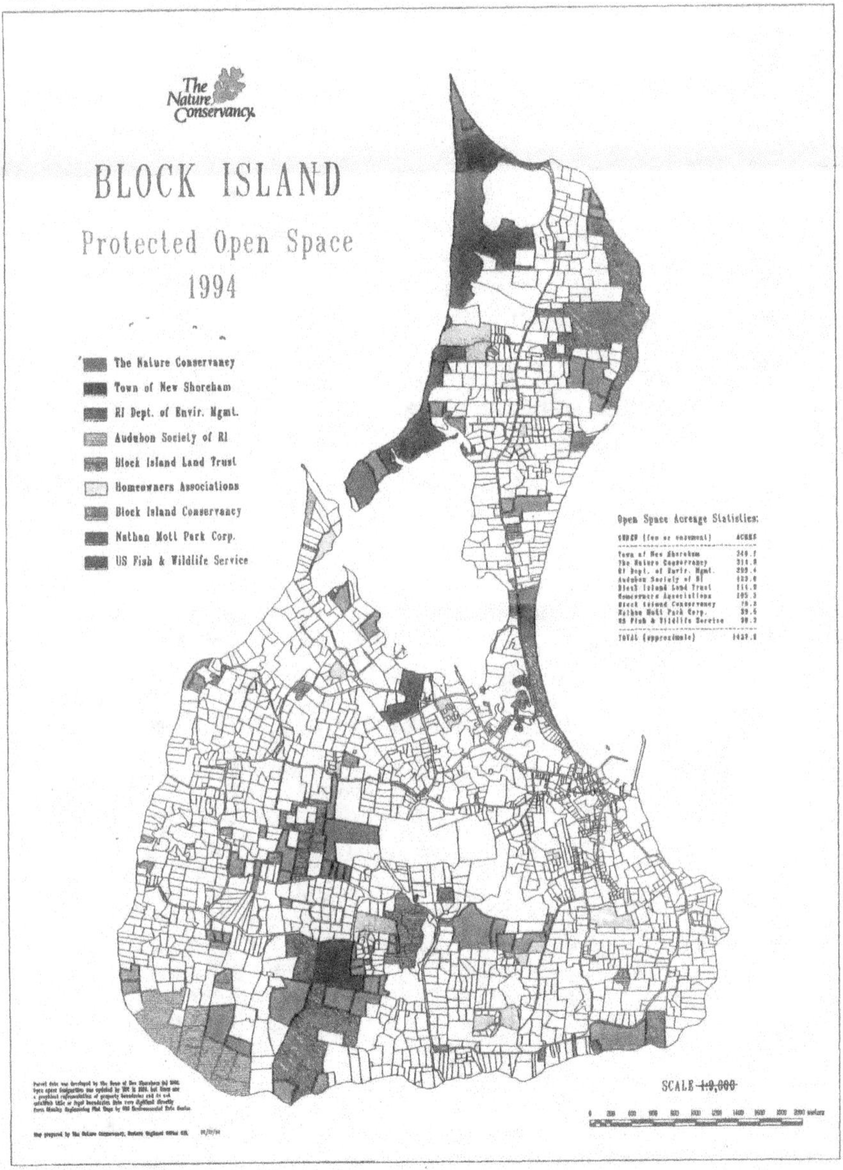

5. Greenwich, Connecticut, a derailed attempt

Equally as instructive as learning of the four on-going municipal open space acquisition programs funded by real estate transfer tax revenues is to review the case of Greenwich, Connecticut where a similar program was proposed and defeated in 1986.

Greenwich is primarily a residential community but also home to many corporate headquarters such as American Brands, US Tobacco, and others. Given its situation some 30 miles from New York City, and 10 from White Plains, New York, it has historically attracted a resident population of executives and families who stay but a few years and then are transferred to new locations. This has been particularly true of IBM employees, and those of several multinational banks. There is no industry in town, but several polo horse farms. The zoning of the 26-square mile town allows for densities from 600 square feet up to one unit per ten acres.

Largely, because there appears to be so much vacant undeveloped land in the larger lot zones, plus a number of 100+ acre properties, the face of the northern sector of town remains predominantly green to the passing eye. But, the passing eye does not take into account that it is because of current zoning restrictions that some of the land is not more densely developed, nor does it take into account that privately-owned properties are always vulnerable to development. Nonetheless, the scenic green view from the car window is apparently sufficient for some.

The Greenwich proposal in fact died even before state enabling legislation was sought. In part, this was a result of affordable housing advocates persuading local officials that it would be politically unwise for them to support an open space preservation proposal. In addition, opposition came from the town's finance officials who voiced extreme reluctance to share any responsibilities for the town's finances with an autonomous open space acquisition program commission, and who viewed bonding as highly undesirable having always practiced the policy of 'pay as you go.' Lastly, some opponents argued against public access to any acquired open parcels, not for ecological considerations, but rather from reluctance in permitting "outsiders" to enjoy the would-be preserved property. Finally, others argued that there already was enough green space (Young 1995).

Conclusion

For a municipal government to attain the goal of acquiring and preserving open space, a number of policy considerations must come into play. One will be the financial cost or the public investment. Will it be all the public through general revenues, or simply a small sector of the public, called on to pay? Advocates of the transfer tax approach would reply that it is fair to assess the activity, namely real estate transfers which are largely responsible for diminishing inventories of open space.

Political ramifications of exactly whom to assess now enter the picture. It is clearly easier to assign a fee to the non-resident and therefore non-voting class of persons, i.e., the buyer. But, is this fair? Does not the remaining resident non-selling population benefit? Will not their land values undoubtedly appreciate by an enhanced landscape and a diminished supply of developable land to buy? The answer must be yes, which is another reason for the political acceptability of such a program. So called 'unearned benefits' are never unpopular at the voting booth. For the voting seller, the picture is equally bright. Almost invariably, he/she will show a profit on the sale of his/her property, a profit substantially over any 'sweat equity' which he/she may have given to the community, a profit realized from factors well beyond his/her control such as thriving economic times or more leisure/vacation opportunities. At least, shouldn't he/she pay? While many might agree with this premise, few would disagree that it is politically easier to enact a fine program for which the faceless someone else i.e., the buyer will pay. So, the question of 'fairness' is superseded by concerns of political feasibility.

Municipal open space acquisition programs such as those discussed in the four case studies promise permanency of preservation. However, such an arrangement does not come without social costs. When developable land is irrevocably removed from the market place, remaining properties escalate in price and are only affordable by the more affluent (Brower and others 1984: 96; Niebanck 1989: 111). However, it does not have to be the case if the property acquired is a wetland, or otherwise unbuildable. An exclusionary environment can be avoided if other provisions are made for the less-affluent to enter the market place. This could be through shared revenues from the transfer tax enabling land purchase or enactment of a dual purpose program where some land is purchased for open space purposes and other property is purchased for affordable housing sites.

CHAPTER FOUR

POLICY ISSUES for CONSIDERATION when DESIGNING a PROGRAM for MUNICIPAL OPEN SPACE ACQUISITION FUNDED by REAL ESTATE TRANSFER TAX REVENUES

The case studies presented in Chapter Three provide models for others seeking to acquire open space in their communities. This chapter presents options available for tailoring a municipal open space acquisition program funded by a real estate transfer tax to fit the specific goals and needs of a community. The following issues for consideration provide a framework within which to categorize the options: timing; purpose; powers; transfer tax; and administration.

Timing

The public's awareness of the need for open space preservation can transform citizens into advocates for municipal land acquisition particularly when they realize that sufficient municipal general funds are unlikely to be appropriated to the cause. The awareness can be heightened in a real estate boom economy which can serve to jump start public appreciation and regret for the diminishing open space inventory within the privately-held sector. As public support from the community is required to approve an open space land banking proposal at the local level, extensive documentation and lobbying is essential to persuade doubters of the efficacy of trying a new approach to address the problem.

Educating about open space values is nothing new for the island communities discussed in Chapter Three; the residents are readily aware. The finiteness and preciousness of land is far more obvious on an island. Even on a large one like Martha's Vineyard, the limiting shore is never more than a long hike or a short ride away (Caputo 1994: 162). Islands have no resources to waste. Their size and natural endowments have required their people to exercise great ingenuity. Keith Lewis, former chairman of the Block Island Land Trust reports, "We've always had a very strong conservation ethic out here. When we came under the threat of overdevelopment, it was natural for the island people to respond and protect the significant areas. We're not against development, but we try to work for sensible development." (Precious 1987: 8).

The islands are alike in having tourism-based economies. Tourists are attracted to the islands because of their open spaces and beaches. Overdevelopment of the islands can threaten tourism. This threat helped promote support for the islands' land acquisition programs. However, a community need not be dependent on tourism to recognize the significance of open space preservation. No matter where the location, open space can enhance the quality of life in any community.

State enabling legislation is required for a community to impose a local real estate transfer tax to fund an open space acquisition program. Proposing this special tax must win approval both at the state and local levels of government. Political support for this proposal may be won or lost at either level. At the local level, resistance may come from affordable housing advocates who view open space preservation as a threat to their cause. The power of land preservation opponents is related by Norma Willis, a former representative in the Rhode Island legislature who unsuccessfully fought for a measure that would have created a municipal open space program (funded by real estate transfer tax revenues) in the town of Jamestown. "The lobbyists really got to the legislature. (Real estate and development lobbyists) said they didn't want the municipal land preservation concept spreading. I think their fear is that communities will try to buy everything in sight, and that's just not realistic," (Precious 1987: 8).

At the state level, the threat is more political in form. Some states already levy a tax on real estate transfers. A state that already has a transfer tax may not be inclined to permit an additional local property transfer tax to be assessed. If an additional transfer tax is permitted, it is virtually assured that there will be protesting voices from one special interest group or another. It might be the real estate lobby, or the construction industry. In the final analysis, public education of the need for open space preservation is the only way to garner sufficient support to overcome the dissident voices.

A better strategy is to initially propose a compromise such as splitting the income received from the transfer tax so that it might be used to provide affordable housing sites, and open space. By working together, goals of both parties can be achieved. Working separately may impede progress.

Purpose

The purpose for a municipal open space acquisition program

funded by a real estate transfer tax should be refined to reflect a community's needs. Therefore, the design of a program should be unique. Following is a guide to issues for consideration when designing the program's purpose: what type of land should be acquired; what kind of interest in land should be acquired; what uses will be permitted; and for what other objectives, if any, the program will hope to achieve.

The type of land to be purchased should be specifically designated. For some communities like Nantucket, beach access is the priority. For others, like Little Compton, farmland protection is given priority. "We just want to maintain some of the rural qualities that make Little Compton a very desirable town to live in," states David Bordon, Chairman of the Little Compton Agricultural Conservancy Trust (Precious 1987: 8).

A municipal open space acquisition program could be restricted to acquisition of land in fee-interest. Or, the purpose could be expanded to include for example, acquisition of development rights. Little Compton again serves as a good example, where purchase of development rights to farmland is given top priority. The Little Compton Agricultural Conservancy Trust provides farmers, a rapidly diminishing segment of the population, a way to continue farming while obtaining money for their valuable land.

A municipal open space acquisition program's purpose should also include a statement on how the how the land is to be used. For instance, should public access be permitted? Ideally the answer should be in the affirmative except in exceedingly well-defined situations where public access might endanger the person or the property or fauna. Denying access is a measure of last resort. Furthermore, questions regarding recreation, passive or active, should also be considered in designing the program's purpose.

If a municipal open space acquisition program is proposed to meet objectives other than conservation, this too should be specified in the statement of purpose. As previously mentioned, a program could be designed to simultaneously provide sites for affordable housing, although this choice puts an obvious strain on funds. But this scenario could mitigate opposition from opponents of open space preservation. The Sakonnet Times, the local paper in Little Compton, reported one dissenting opinion from resident Deborah Sullivan, "I feel that they're making it more difficult for young people to stay in Town" (1994).

Powers

The minimum powers of a commission administrating a municipal open space acquisition program funded by a real estate transfer tax should include the authority to purchase land using funds collected from a real estate transfer tax. The commission should also be empowered to receive gifts. The commission could also receive fees in lieu of the 15% land reservations required in the subdivision process as the local zoning commission might deem appropriate, on a case by case basis. At its discretion, a community may also seek to empower a commission to exercise eminent domain, incur debt and issue bonds, on a case by case basis. The public should be afforded the opportunity to speak before any action is taken either to involuntarily secure property from land owners, or to issue bonds pledging the full faith and credit of the community.

Bonds have been used to assist the Nantucket Land Bank purchasing activities with the Town of Nantucket placing its full faith and credit behind the bonds. Since its inception in 1984, real estate sales have dropped, and with them real estate transfer tax revenues. In response the Nantucket Land Bank has come to rely on issuing highly secure, AAA bonds. These resources provided the means to acquiring critical parcels of land before the property was lost to development (Stolz 1990: 26).

Empowering a commission with special authority does not necessarily mean that the authority will be exercised. The Martha's Vineyard Land Bank Commission may use eminent domain, but it has not done so, as yet. Again when queried on the subject, James Lengyel Executive Director of the Martha's Vineyard Land Bank Commission stated, "No we've never used it, and the answer will be the same in the year 2050" (1995). As previously mentioned, use of eminent domain could well prove damaging to a program's public relations.

Transfer tax

The communities discussed in the case studies have chosen to use the term "transfer fee" or "conveyance fee" instead of transfer tax to describe how each municipal open space acquisition program is funded. The word "tax" can have negative connotations. Whatever term is chosen, the essential features of the transfer tax include: rate; who would pay the tax; exemptions; and termination date (sunset provision) for the tax. A community has some flexibility in designing these features.

Enabling legislation for the programs discussed in Chapter Three, permit taxing at a rate up to 5% of the total purchase price of property. Imposing a rate greater than 5% may incur opposition. In recent years, proposals have been made to reduce the 2% tax rate in Little Compton, but each year Towns people strike down this initiative (Eddy 1994). In contrast, the Block Island Land Trust in 1989, successfully raised their tax rate from 2 to 3% (Tarbox 1995).

It is questionable who should pay the tax, the purchaser or the seller. Usually, conveyance taxes are paid by the buyer. This is how the four programs discussed in Chapter Three are structured. However, a strong argument can be made for payment by the seller. Although their program's proposal was later defeated, the report of the Town of Greenwich, Connecticut, Selectman's Land Bank Committee is persuasive in recommending that the purchaser pay the tax:

> Present residents and taxpayers have made their contributions to the Town - the taxes they've paid have maintained the appeal of the Town over the years through its high level of municipal services, its fine schools and its protection of the environment. The purchasers of property should contribute to a Land Bank because they have a greater stake than the sellers in preserving the essential qualities of the Town (1986: 16).

The purchaser can consider the tax an indication of the community's commitment to protect existing desirable character. This makes buying into a community with a municipal open space acquisition program an attractive investment. Again, in Nantucket, those who are required to pay the tax do not complain, reports Nantucket Land Bank director Dawn Darbey-Dugan. "We tell them, 'This is your insurance policy, this is going to protect your home.' People don't object. They understand the land bank is for their children" (Stolz 1990: 27).

Waivers from the tax can be given to those involved in real-estate transfers unlikely to produce new development, such as inheritances, marital divisions, and transfers to religious and charitable organizations. Exemptions for first-time home buyers should also be considered. An extra 2 or 3% added to the total purchase price of land could exclude some home buyers. A waiver from the tax is provided, for a portion of the total purchase price, by the four existing programs discussed in Chapter Three.

A "sunset" provision or termination clause, may also be included in a program's proposal. It might seem right to give a community the opportunity to terminate collection of the tax when, in its judgment, it is appropriate to do so. However, this decision should be made cautiously. If the tax were to be terminated, this would most seriously impair any power of a open space acquisition program to borrow against its future revenues. Without funding from the tax, and the consequential elimination of borrowing power, a program may become disabled.

Administration

Consideration should be given to who would govern a municipal open space acquisition program (funded by a real estate transfer tax). As illustrated in the case studies, a commission is usually formed to manage a program, the members of which are either elected or appointed. If local public officials are inclined to engage in a power struggle (as was the case in the Town of Greenwich, Connecticut), communities may find it politically more acceptable to permit existing local legislative bodies to appoint program administrators. Alternatively, Nantucket chose an elective body for its land bank commission because the benefits of accountability to the voters were believed to outweigh the need for political autonomy (Melious 1986: 44).

The Little Compton Agricultural Conservancy Trust demonstrates a unique approach to the membership issue. At least one member must be an active farmer. This decision is appropriate for an agricultural community. In addition to choosing commission members by election or appointment, an existing board such as the local conservation commission could be empowered to administer a program.

No matter what their title, commission members should have a working knowledge of land management practices so that they can draft an open space plan to guide their work and manage the properties under their program's jurisdiction. New technologies may also be of aid in this task. For example, the Block Island Land Trust used BIGIS (Block Island Geographic Information System) and ARC/INFO (a GIS software) to develop their open space management plan and to target desirable tracts of land for acquisition.

Commission members will bear the responsibility also of

formulating maintenance programs for each property and financially accepting the stewardship responsibilities. For these tasks they may choose to hire qualified personnel.

CHAPTER FIVE

CONCLUSION

It is relatively easy for most American communities to define their character and chart their desired future. It is more difficult for policy makers serving on a local planning and zoning commission to maintain the special character of their town in the face of continued urbanizing pressures.

Regulatory zoning powers alone are now viewed as insufficient to implement the objective of preserving strategically located areas of open space. Neither reliance on further restriction of individual property rights nor occasional land donations will adequately preserve critical open space areas. Furthermore, there is risk involved with a town depending on local and non-local non-profit land conservation organizations to do the job. Therefore, a program funded by a real estate transfer tax enabling a community to acquire key open space lands with an assured source of funding in the open market is most attractive.

The study suggests that generating revenues for open space acquisition through a real estate transfer tax is a logical approach to environmental planning. When using this approach where there is the most active real estate market, as a beneficial consequence the greatest amount of funds will be realized. Environmental protection is provided for at a level directly related to the need. Political support for program's proposal would therefore most likely be gained in those communities experiencing an increase in real estate market activity.

This study has emphasized the importance of designing a municipal open space acquisition program (funded by a real estate transfer tax) to reflect local needs. For other communities who are considering such a proposal, I highly recommend a proscriptive study be completed so that problems can be identified and anticipated, before a vote is cast. Representatives from local community groups should be invited to participate in any preliminary discussions. Conservationists, affordable housing advocates, realtors, and many more can be relied upon to have an opinion on such a proposal. However, time like open space should not be wasted. Debates are sure to continue, but at what cost? In the mean time, open space is being lost to development.

This study may persuade citizens to attempt establishing a municipal open space acquisition program funded by a real estate transfer tax in their community. To do so, the following actions are required: Acceptance by the governing body of the municipality; authorization by the state legislature to enable the town to impose a tax; and ratification by the local electorate. An advocate should, therefore:

- Formulate the program to fit the town;
- Have the selected program adopted by town meeting, or mayor and city council;
- Submit the bill to a state representative or senator for passage by the state legislature and lobby for its passage;
- Campaign to have the referendum question/warrant article ratified by a majority of the local voters.

Municipal open space acquisition funded by a real estate transfer tax is not a panacea, but it offers a means for a community to cooperatively determine its priority properties, and then save and/or borrow if necessary to acquire them when they become available. This really becomes an object lesson is a community defining its own destiny.

It is certain that no magic formula exists to acquire and preserve meaningful areas of open space for community enjoyment that will be without its critics. Nonetheless, having considered some traditional and non-traditional methods, it is instructive to read a recent article in Small Town, by Sara Briles who advances an alternative approach to the issue. Unlike municipal open space acquisition programs and different from conservancy land trusts whose avowed purpose is to protect fragile or ecologically important natural areas, "A community land trust can also incorporate conservancy uses, but its primary purpose is to provide uses associated with daily human life: housing, schools, play areas, shopping, civic infrastructure and work-related facilities" (Briles 1995: 19).

This visionary idea has been translated into actuality since the passage in June 1987 of the Vermont Housing and Conservation Trust Fund Act. Utilizing over $75 million in state money gained from surplus funds, transfer tax revenues and outright state appropriations plus an additional $180 million leveraged from other public and private sources, the program has provided funding for projects in 175 Vermont towns both for affordable housing and conservation needs.

Additionally, an active program for the purchase of development rights on agricultural land and managed forest land has been initiated under this Act. Since the program's inception, over 3,500 affordable housing units have been provided and development rights purchased on more than 41,000 acres of farm land permitting less onerous intergenerational transfers of working farms (1995 Vermont Housing and Conservation Board Report to the General Assembly).

Forging a coalition between what many perceive to be disparate interests in land use has been the hallmark of the Vermont success story. The spirit of cooperative effort and the willingness of the Vermont citizenry to acknowledge that land and money supplies are finite, and that no one cause deserves exclusive use of same characterizes the achievements of the program. Whether this represents a more generally applicable approach than municipal open space acquisition funded by a real estate transfer tax as practiced in a few island communities will be for other towns and states to determine in the future.

For those who believe that there remains sufficient time and a sufficient number of "other" people to worry about preserving open space, it is unlikely that any municipal land preservation program will be established in their community. But for those who look about at familiar landscape and see tract houses rising over once cherished corn fields or obscuring favorite views and who galvanize their fellow citizens "to do something;" for them the outlook may be brighter.

THE COMMONWEALTH OF MASSACHUSETTS

CHAPTER 669 Acts and Resolves

In the Year One Thousand Nine Hundred Eighty-Three

An Act RELATIVE TO THE NANTUCKET ISLANDS LAND BANK

Be it enacted by the Senate and House of Representatives in General Court assembled, and by the authority of the same, as follows:

SECTION 1. For purposes of this act, the words and phrases set forth in this section shall have the following meanings:

"Commission", shall refer to the Nantucket Islands Land Bank Commission, established by section three.

"Fund", shall refer to the Nantucket Islands Land Bank Fund, established under the provisions of section eight.

"Institutional lender", any bank defined in section one of chapter one hundred and sixty-seven of the General Laws, any insurance company defined in section one of chapter one hundred and seventy-five of the General Laws, and any mortgage company or investment company that made more than twenty mortgages in the calendar year preceding the year of the relevant mortgage for the purposes of subsection (m) of section twelve, and any national bank, federal savings and loan association, federal savings bank, bank holding company, or state or federally chartered credit union.

"Land bank", the Nantucket Islands Land Bank, established by section two.

"Purchaser", the transferee, grantee or recipient of any real property interests.

"Purchase price", all consideration paid or transferred by or on behalf of a purchaser to a seller or his nominee, or for his benefit, for the transfer of any real property interest, and shall include, but not be limited to, all cash or its equivalent so paid or transferred; all cash or other property paid or transferred by or on behalf of the purchaser to discharge or reduce any obligation of the seller; the principal amount of all notes or their equivalent, or other deferred payments, given or promised to be given by or on behalf of the purchaser to the seller or his nominee; the outstanding balance of all obligations of the seller which are assumed by the purchaser or to which the real property interest transferred remains subject after the transfer, determined at the time of transfer, but excluding real estate taxes and other municipal liens or assessments which are not overdue at the time of transfer; the the fair market value, at the time of transfer, of any other consideration or thing of value paid or transferred by or on behalf of the purchaser, including, but not limited to, any property, goods or services paid, transferred or rendered in exchange for such real property interest.

"Real property interest", any present or future legal or equitable interest in or to real property, and any beneficial interest therein, including the interest of any beneficiary in a trust which holds any legal or equitable interest in real property; but shall not include any interest which is limited to any or all of the following: the dominant estate in any easement or right of way; the right to enforce any restriction; any estate at will or at sufferance, and any estate for years having a term of less than thirty years; any reversionary right, condition, or right of entry for condition broken; the interest of a mortgage or other secured party in any mortgage or security agreement; and the interest of a stockholder in a corporation, or a partner in a partnership.

"Seller", the transferor, grantor or immediate former owner of any real property interests.

"Time of transfer", of any real property interest shall mean, the time at which such transfer is legally effective as between the parties thereto, and, in any event, with respect to a transfer evidenced by an instrument recorded with the appropriate registry of deeds or filed with the assistant recorder of the appropriate registry district, not later than the time of such recording or filing.

St.1983, c.669, s.1.

SECTION 2. There is hereby established a Nantucket Islands Land Bank, to be administered by a commission established by section three, for the purpose of acquiring, holding and managing land and interests in land of the types set forth in section five. The land bank is hereby constituted a body politic and corporate and a public instrumentality and the exercise of powers herein conferred upon the land bank shall be deemed to be the performance of an essential governmental function.

St.1983, c.669, s.2. Amended by St.1984, c.407, s.1.

Historical note

St.1984, c.407, s.1 added the second sentence.

SECTION 3. The land bank shall be administered by a Commission consisting of five persons elected for staggered five-year terms; and provided that the county commissioners of Nantucket county shall appoint the initial five persons forthwith upon acceptance of this act, to serve until the first annual election of the members to be held at the first annual town election following the acceptance of this act. Members shall be legal residents of Nantucket county and shall serve without compensation. The Commission shall elect a chairman and a secretary/treasurer, from among its members, and may adopt reasonable rules and regulations for the conduct of its affairs and the management of its holdings not inconsistent with the provisions of this act. Decisions of the Commission shall be by majority vote of those present and voting and no business shall be transacted without three members present. The Commission shall keep accurate records of its meetings and actions and shall file an annual report which shall be printed in the annual town report.

St.1983, c.669, s.3.

SECTION 4. The Commission shall, subject to the provisions of this act, have the power and authority to (a) purchase and acquire fee simple interests, and any lesser interests, in any land in Nantucket county, of the types set forth in section five, including any improvements thereon; (b) accept gifts of any such interests in land, or of funds to further the purposes of the Land bank; (c) take any such interests in land by eminent domain pursuant to chapter seventy-nine of the General Laws, and only by a vote of the Commission in which at least four members vote in favor of such taking and further only after having been authorized to do so in each instance by a two-thirds vote of an annual town meeting of the town of Nantucket, and further provided that a reasonable effort shall first be made to negotiate the acquisition thereof by purchase prior to such taking; (d) dispose of all or any portion of its interests in any land or interests thereon held by it, subject to the provisions of Article XCVII of the articles of amendments to the Constitution of Massachusetts to the extent applicable; (e) incur debt, pledging the full faith and credit of the town of Nantucket or of Nantucket county, or of both, only after having been authorized to do so in each instance by a two-thirds vote of a town meeting of the town of Nantucket; (f) hire such staff and obtain such professional services as are necessary in order to perform its duties; (g) administer and manage land and interests in land held by it in a manner which allows public use and enjoyment consistent with the natural and scenic resources thereof; (h) lease real property as may be held by the Land bank for purposes consistent with this act; and (i) finance and construct recreational facilities, subject to the provisions of section six.

St.1983, c.669, s.4. Amended by St.1987, c.666, s.1.

Historical Note

St.1987, c.666, s.1 added (h) and (i) to section 4.

SECTION 4A. The Town of Nantucket is hereby authorized to appropriate money to be deposited in the Nantucket islands land bank fund as provided in section eight and to provide funds to repay notes of the town issued pursuant to section four C and, when authorized by a two-thirds vote as defined in section one of chapter forty-four of the General Laws, to incur debt of the town for such purposes in accordance with the provisions of clause (3) of section seven of said chapter forty-four.

St.1984, c.407, s.2

SECTION 4B. The land bank is hereby empowered to issue its bonds and notes, including notes in anticipation of bonds, for the purpose of acquiring land and interests in land as provided in section four. The proceeds of such bonds or notes may be used to pay, in whole or in part, acquisition costs; to provide reserves for debt service and other expenses; to pay consulting, appraisal, advisory and legal fees and costs incidental to the issuance and sale of such bonds or notes; to purchase, refund or renew bonds or notes previously issued; and to pay any other costs and expenses of the land bank necessary for the accomplishment of its purposes. Bonds or notes issued under this act shall be authorized by the Commission which shall have full power and authority to determine the amount, form, terms, conditions, provisions for the payment of interest and all other details thereof and to provide for their sale and issuance at such price and in such manner as the Commission shall determine, subject only to any limitations set forth in this act. Unless the town of Nantucket shall have authorized by a two-thirds vote of a town meeting the pledging of the full faith and credit of the town of Nantucket or of Nantucket county to secure an issue of bonds or notes of the land bank, all bonds or notes issued hereunder shall be payable solely from the fees and other revenues of the land bank pledged to their payment and shall not be deemed a pledge of the full faith and credit of the town or county of Nantucket, the commonwealth or any political subdivision therein.

The Commission may enter into any agreements, including without limitation a loan agreement and a trust agreement, necessary to effectuate and to secure any bonds or notes issued by the land bank. Such agreements may pledge or assign, in whole or in part, the revenues and other money held or to be received by the land bank. Such agreements may contain such provisions for protecting and enforcing the rights, security and remedies of the holders of such bonds or notes, including, without limiting the generality of the foregoing, provisions defining defaults and providing for remedies in the event thereof which may include the acceleration of maturities and covenants setting forth the duties of, and limitations on, the land bank in relation to the custody, safeguarding, investment and application of money, the issuance of additional debt obligations, the use of any surplus proceeds of the borrowing, including any investment earnings thereon, and establishment of special funds and reserves.

The pledge of any such agreement shall be valid and binding and shall be deemed continuously perfected for the purposes of the Uniform Commercial Code from the time when the pledge is made; the revenues, money, rights and proceeds so pledged and then held or thereafter acquired or received by the land bank shall immediately be subject to the lien of such pledge without any physical delivery or segregation thereof or further act; and the lien of any such pledge shall be valid and binding against all parties having claims of any kind in tort, contract or otherwise against the town or county, irrespective of whether such parties have notice thereof. No document by which a pledge is created need be filed or recorded except in the records of the land bank and no filing need by made under the Uniform Commercial Code.

The trustee with respect to any such trust agreement entered into pursuant to this section shall be a trust company or a bank having the powers of a trust company within the commonwealth. Any such trust agreement may provide that any money received thereunder may be held, deposited or invested by the trustee, notwithstanding the provisions of section eight, pending the disbursement thereof, in any deposits or investments which are lawful for the funds of savings banks and shall provide that any officer with whom or any bank or trust company with which such money shall be deposited shall act as trustee of such money and shall hold and apply the same for the purposes hereof and thereof, subject to such regulation or limitation as this act or such trust agreement may provide.

It shall be lawful for any bank or trust company within the commonwealth to act as depository of the proceeds of bonds or notes, revenues or other money hereunder and to furnish such indemnifying bonds or to pledge such security, if any, as may be required by the Commission. Any trust agreement entered into pursuant to this section may set forth the rights and remedies of the holders of any bonds or notes and of the trustee and may restrict the individual rights of action by any such holders. In addition to the foregoing, any such trust agreement may contain such other provisions as the Commission may deem reasonable and proper. All expenses incurred in carrying out the provisions of such trust agreement may be treated as part of the cost of operation of the land bank and paid from the revenues or other funds pledged or assigned to the payment of the principal of the the premium, if any, and interest on the bonds or notes or from any other funds available to the land bank. In addition to other security provided herein or otherwise by law, bonds or notes issued under this section may be secured, in whole or in part, by insurance or by letters or lines of credit or other credit facilities issued to the land bank by any bank, trust company or other financial institution, within or without the commonwealth, and the land bank may pledge or assign any of its revenues as security for the reimbursement by the land bank to the issuers of such letters or lines of credit, insurance or credit facilities of any payments made thereunder.

St.1984, c.407, s.2.

SECTION 4C. If at any time any principal or interest is due or about to come due on any bonds or notes of the land bank to secure which the full faith and credit of the town of Nantucket or Nantucket county shall have been pledged and funds to pay the same are not available, the Commission shall certify to the town treasurer and selectmen of the town or to the county treasurer and county commissioners of the county, as appropriate, the amount required to meet such obligations and the town treasurer or the county treasurer shall thereupon pay over to the land bank the amount so certified from any funds in the treasury. For the purpose of providing or restoring to the treasury the sums so paid over to the land bank, the town treasurer, with the approval of the selectmen, is authorized to incur debt outside the town's debt limit and issue notes therefor for a period not exceeding two years and to renew or refund the same from time to time until the town shall have received from the land bank sufficient funds to repay such notes and the interest thereon in full. Whenever the town or the county shall have been required to pay over any sums of money to the land bank under this section, the land bank shall be precluded from acquiring any additional property, or issuing any of its bonds or notes for purposes other than repaying the town, until the land bank shall have repaid the town in full for all sums paid to the land bank hereunder, including interest on any notes issued for such purpose, unless the town shall have appropriated sufficient funds for such purpose at a town meeting.

St.1984, c.407, s.2.

SECTION 4D. Bonds and notes issued under the provisions of this act are hereby made securities in which all public officers and public bodies of the commonwealth and its political subdivisions, all insurance companies, trust companies in their commercial departments, savings banks, cooperative banks, banking associations, investment companies, executors, administrators, trustees and other fiduciaries may properly and legally invest funds, including capital in their control or belonging to them. Such bonds and notes are hereby made securities which may properly and legally be deposited with and received by any state or municipal officer or any agency or political subdivision of the commonwealth for any purpose for which the deposit of bonds or obligations of the commonwealth is now or may hereafter be authorized by law.

St.1984, c.407, s.2.

SECTION 4E. Notwithstanding any of the provisions of this act or any recitals in any bonds or notes issued under this act, all such bonds and notes shall be deemed to be investment securities under the Uniform Commercial Code.

St.1984, c.407, s.2.

SECTION 4F. Bonds and notes may be issued under this act without obtaining the consent of any department, division, commission, board, bureau or agency of the town or county of Nantucket, except that the full faith and credit of the town or county of Nantucket shall not be pledged for the payment of such bonds or notes unless such pledge shall have been authorized by a two-thirds vote as provided in section four, and without any other proceedings or the happening of any other conditions or things than those proceedings, conditions or things which are specifically required therefor by this act. The validity of and security for any bonds and notes issued by the land bank shall not be affected by the existence or nonexistence of any such consent or other proceedings, conditions or things.

St.1984, c.407, s.2.

SECTION 4G. The land bank and all its revenues, income and real and personal property used solely by the land bank in furtherance of its public purposes shall be exempt from taxation and from betterments and special assessments and the land bank shall not be required to pay any tax, excise or assessment to or for the commonwealth or any of its political subdivisions. Bonds and notes issued by the land bank, their transfer and the income therefrom, including any profit made on the sale thereof, shall at all times be exempt from taxation within the commonwealth.

St.1984, c.407, s.2

SECTION 5. Land to be acquired and held as part of the land bank, or interests in which are to be so acquired and held, shall be situated in Nantucket county. and may consist of any of the following types of land and interests therein; (a) ocean, harbor and pond frontage in the form of beaches, dunes and adjoining backlands; (b) barrier beaches; (c) fresh and salt water marshes, estuaries and adjoining uplands; (d) heathland and moors; (e) land providing access to ocean, harbor and pond frontage and land for bicycle paths; (f) land for future public recreational facilities and use; (g) recreation land to protect existing and future wellfields and aquifer recharge areas; and (h) land used or to be used for agricultural purposes.

St.1983, c.669, s.1. Amended by St.1987, c.666, s.2.

Historical Note

St.1987, c.666, s.2 added (h).

SECTION 6. The commission shall retain any real property interest relating to land and water areas acquired pursuant to this act predominantly in it natural, scenic or open condition except as provided for by this section. Except upon the approval of the secretary of environmental affairs and where appropriate, subject to the general laws, any special law, or the constitution of Massachusetts, the commission shall not allow (a)construction or placing of buildings, roads, signs, billboards, or other advertising utilities or other structures on or above the surface, (b) dumping or placing of soil or other substance or material as landfill, or dumping or placing of trash, waste or unsightly or offensive materials, (c) removal or destruction of trees, shrubs, or other vegetation, (d) excavation, dredging, or removal of loam, peat, gravel, soil, rock, or other mineral substance in such manner as to affect the surface, (e) surface use except for purposes permitting the land or water area to remain predominantly in its natural condition, (f) activities detrimental to drainage, flood control, water conservation, erosion control, or soil conservation, or (g) other acts or uses detrimental to such retention of land or water areas. In determining whether or not to approve a request from the commission to use, improve or dispose of any real property interest acquired by said commission in a manner otherwise prohibited by this section, the secretary shall consider whether such request is in the interest of conservation and any natural, state, regional or local program in furtherance thereof, and also any public, state, regional or local comprehensive land use or development plan affecting the land, and any known proposal by a governmental body for use of the land.

St.1983, c.669, s.6.

SECTION 7. The Commission shall file annually with the secretary of environmental affairs a conservation, public access, and outdoor recreation plan which shall be, as far as possible, consistent with the town master plan and with any regional planning relating to the area. The Commission may, from time to time, amend such plan. The plan shall show all real property interests then currently held by the Commission including a description of the use thereof, and all acquisitions, improvements or dispositions of real property interests held by the Commission at any time during the year preceding each filing, including the reasons for such acquisition, improvement or disposition; the secretary of environmental affairs may require any other information he deems important.

St.1983, c.669,s.7.

SECTION 8. The Commission shall meet its financial obligations by drawing upon a Nantucket islands land bank fund, to be set up as a revolving or sinking account within the treasury of Nantucket county. Deposits into the fund shall include (a) funds appropriated to be deposited into the fund by vote of the county commissioners of Nantucket county or of a town meeting of the town of Nantucket; (b) voluntary contributions of money and other liquid assets to the fund; (c) revenues from fees imposed upon the transfer of real property interests as set forth in section ten occurring after the effective date of this act as set forth in section fifteen, together with payments of interest and penalties under section thirteen, and (d) proceeds from disposal of real property or interests. All expenses lawfully incurred by the Commission in carrying out the provisions of this act shall be evidenced by proper vouchers and shall be paid by the county treasurer only upon submission of warrants duly approved by the Commission. The county treasurer of said county shall prudently invest available assets of the fund, and all income thereon shall accrue to the fund. Real property held in the name of the Nantucket Islands land bank or its designee shall be exempt from property taxes as of the date of the acquisition of title by the Nantucket Islands land bank or its designee; and any taxes assessed against such real property interests shall be abated for that portion of any fiscal year during which the real property interests was owned by the Nantucket Islands land bank or its designee.

St.1983, c.669, s.8. Amended by St.1987, c.666, s.3.

Historical Note

St.1987, c.666, s.3 added the last sentence.

SECTION 9. The Commission shall keep a full and accurate account of its actions including a record as to when, from or to whom, and on what account money has been paid or received relative to this act, and as to when, from and to whom and for what consideration real property interests have been acquired, improved, or disposed of. Said records and accounts shall be subject to examination by the director of accounts or his agent pursuant to section forty-five of chapter thirty-five of the General Laws.

The county treasurer shall keep a full and accurate account stating when, from or to whom, and on what account money has been paid or received relative to the activities of the commission and the land bank. Said account shall be subject to examination by the director of accounts or his agent pursuant to section forty-four of chapter thirty-five of the General Laws.

St.1983, c.669, s.9.

SECTION 10. There is hereby imposed a fee equal to two per cent of the purchase price upon the transfer of any real property interest in any real property situated in Nantucket county. Said fee shall be the liability of the purchaser of such real property interest, and any agreement between the purchaser and the seller or any other person with reference to the allocation of the responsibility for bearing said fee shall not affect such liability of the purchaser. The fee shall be paid to the Commission, or its designee, and shall be accompanied by a copy of the deed or other instrument evidencing such transfer, if any, and an affidavit signed under oath or under the pains and penalties of perjury by the purchaser or his legal representative, attesting to the true and complete purchase price and the basis, if any, upon which the transfer is claimed to be exempt in whole or in part from the fee imposed hereby. The Commission, or its designee, shall promptly thereafter execute and issue a certificate indicating that the appropriate fee has been paid or that the transfer is exempt from the fee, stating the basis for the exemption. The register of deeds for Nantucket county, and the assistant recorder for the registry district of Nantucket county, shall not record or register, or receive or accept for recording or registration, any deed, except a mortgage deed, to which has not been affixed such a certificate executed by the commission or its designee. Failure to comply with this requirement shall not affect the validity of any instrument. The commission shall deposit all fees received hereunder with the county treasurer of Nantucket county, as a part of the fund established by section eight. The fee imposed hereunder shall be due simultaneously with the time of transfer of the transfer upon which it is imposed. Notwithstanding the foregoing, whenever there is a conveyance of real property interests and a conveyance of personalty related thereto at or about the same time, the allocations of payments between real estate and personalty agreed to by the purchaser and seller shall not determine the amount of the fee due pursuant to this section; instead, the commission may require payment of the fee referred to in real property interests so conveyed as determined by the commission.

St.1983, c.669, s.10. Amended by St.1987, c.666, s.4

Historical Note

St.1987, c.666, s.4 added last sentence to section 10.

SECTION 10A. To the extent not otherwise subject to payment of a fee pursuant to section ten, and notwithstanding the exemptions set forth in paragraphs (i) and (j) of section twelve, unless otherwise exempted pursuant to section twelve excluding said paragraphs (i) and (j), there shall be paid a fee equal to two per cent of the fair market value of real property interests held in the name of or otherwise owned by a corporation upon the transfer by the controlling stockholders of their interests of the stock of such corporation. This fee is due on or before the time of transfer of the stock.

To the extent not otherwise subject to payment of a fee pursuant to section ten and notwithstanding the exemptions referred to in said paragraphs (i) and (j), unless otherwise exempted pursuant to said section twelve excluding said paragraphs (i) and (j), there shall be paid a fee equal to two per cent of the fair market value of real property interests held in the name of a partnership or otherwise owned by a partnership upon the change in composition of such partnership either in one transaction or a series of related transactions which change in composition results in a transfer of capital interests in excess of fifty per cent of the total capital interests within such partnerships or results in a transfer of the ownership rights to profit interests within such partnership in excess of fifty per cent of the total profit interests within such partnerships.

St.1987, c.666, s.5.

SECTION 11. At any time within seven days following the issuance of the certificate of payment of the fee imposed by section ten, the purchaser or his legal representative may return said certificate to the Commission or its designee for cancellation, together with an affidavit signed under oath or under the pains and penalties of perjury that the transfer, with respect to which such certificate was issued, has not been consummated, and thereupon the fee paid with respect to such transfer shall be forthwith returned to the purchaser or his legal representative.

St.1983, c.669, s.11.

SECTION 12. The following transfers of real property interests shall be exempt from the fee established by section ten. Except as otherwise provided, the purchaser shall have the burden of proof that any transfer is exempt hereunder.

(a) Transfers to the government of the United States, the commonwealth, and any of their instrumentalities, agencies or subdivisions.

(b) Transfers which, without additional consideration, confirm, correct, modify or supplement a transfer previously made.

(c) Transfers made as gifts without consideration. In any proceeds to determine the amount of any fee due hereunder, it shall be presumed that any transfer for consideration of less than fair market value of the real property interests transferred and the amount of consideration claimed by the purchaser to have been paid or transferred, if the purchaser shall have been at the time of transfer the spouse, the lineal descendant, or the lineal ancestor of the seller, by blood or adoption, and otherwise it shall be presumed that consideration was paid in an amount equal to the fair market value of the real property interests transferred, at the time of transfer.

(d) Transfer to the trustees of a trust in exchange for a beneficial interest received by the seller in such trust; distributions by the trustees of a trust to the beneficiaries of such trust.

(e) Transfers by operation of law without actual consideration, including but not limited to transfers occurring by virtue of the death or bankruptcy of the owner of a real property interest.

(f) Transfers made in partition of land and improvements thereto, under chapter two hundred and forty-one of the General Laws.

(g) Transfers to any charitable organization as defined in clause Third of section five of chapter fifty-nine of the General Laws, or any religious organization, provided that the real property interests so transferred will be held by the charitable or religious organization solely for its public charitable or religious purposes.

(h) Transfers to a mortgagee in foreclosure of the mortgage held by such mortgagee, and transfers of the property subject to a mortgage to the mortgagee in consideration of the forbearance of the mortgagee from foreclosing said mortgage.

(i) Transfers made to a corporation or partnership at the time of its formation, pursuant to which transfer no gain or loss is recognized under the provisions of section three hundred and fifty-one of the Internal Revenue Code of 1954, as amended; provided, however, that such transfer shall be exempt only in the event that (i) with respect to a corporation, the transferor retains a controlling interest in such corporation after such formation or (ii), with respect to a partnership, the transferor retains after such formation rights to capital interests in excess of fifty per cent of the capital interests within such partnership or retains rights to profit interests within such partnership in excess of fifty per cent of the total profit interests within such partnership.

(j) Transfers made to a stockholder of a corporation in liquidation of the corporation, and transfers made to a partner of a partnership in dissolution of the partnership; provided, however, that such transfer shall be exempt only in the event that (i) with respect to a corporation, the transferee had prior to the transfer a controlling interest in such corporation or (ii) with respect to a partnership, the transferee had prior to the transfer rights to capital interests in excess of fifty per cent of the total capital interests within such partnership or had rights to profit interests within such partnership in excess of fifty per cent of the total profit interests within such partnership.

(k) Transfers consisting of the division of marital assets under the provisions of section thirty-four of chapter two hundred and eight of the General Laws or other provisions of law.

(l) Transfers of property consisting in part of real property interests situated in Nantucket county and in part of other property interests, to the extent that the property transferred consists of property other than real property situated in Nantucket county; provided that the purchaser shall furnish the Commission with such information as it shall require or request in support of the claim of exemption and manner of allocation of the consideration for such transfers.

(m) The first one hundred thousand dollars of the purchase price of a transfer made to a purchaser who, or whose spouse at the time of transfer, has at no time prior to said transfer owned or possessed any real property interest as defined in section one either within or without Nantucket county; provided that the purchaser shall make the real property interest which is the subject of the transfer the purchaser's actual domicile within two years of the time of transfer; provided further that in the event of a subsequent transfer within five years of the transfer exempted from the fee under this subsection, other than the transfer of a mortgage to an institutional lender, the fee exempted shall become due, together with the accumulated interest and penalties, and in addition to any fee otherwise due as a result of the subsequent transfer. The purchaser shall certify as to the foregoing, and the Commission shall attach to the deed a certificate which shall recite the fact that there is running with the land a lien equal to the amount of the fee exempted plus accumulated interest and penalties until such time as all conditions of this subsection have been met.

St.1983, c.669, s.12. Amended by St.1984, c.407, s.3 and St.1987, c.666, ss.6,7,8.

Historical Note

St.1984, c.407, s.3 extended the amount of time allowed before domicile requirement from one year to two years (line 7) and deleted "with the intention to remain permanently or for an indefinite time and without any certain purpose to return to a former place of abode."

St.1987, c.666, s.6 added to (i):"; provided, however, that such transfer shall be exempt only in the event that (i) with respect to a corporation, the transferor retains a controlling interest in such corporation after such formation or (ii), with respect to a partnership, the transferor retains after such formation rights to capital interests in excess of fifty per cent of the capital interests within such partnership or retains rights to profit interests within such partnership in excess of fifty per cent of the total profit interests within such partnership."

St.1987, c.666, s.7 added to (j): "; provided, however, that such transfer shall be exempt only in the event that (i) with respect to a corporation, the transferee had prior to the transfer a controlling interest in such corporation or (ii) with respect to a partnership, the transferee had prior to the transfer rights to capital interests in excess of fifty per cent of the total capital interests within such partnership or had rights to profit interests within such partnership in excess of fifty per cent of the total profit interests within such partnership."

St.1987, c.666, s.8 amended (m) by substituting the word "shall" for "intends to" on line 6.

SECTION 13. A purchaser who fails to pay all or any portion of the fee established by section ten on or before the time when the same is due shall be liable for the following additional payments in addition to said fee:

(a) Interest: The purchaser shall pay interest on the unpaid amount of the fee to be calculated from the time of transfer at a rate equal to fourteen per cent per annum.

(b) Penalties: Any person who, without fraud or willful intent to defeat or evade a fee imposed by this chapter, fails to pay all or a portion of the fee within thirty days after the time of transfer, shall pay a penalty equal to five per cent of the outstanding fee as determined by the Commission for each month or portion thereof thereafter that the fee is not paid in full; provided, however, that in no event shall the amount of any penalty imposed hereunder exceed twenty-five per cent of the unpaid fee due at the time of transfer. Whenever the Commission determines that all or a portion of a fee due under this chapter was unpaid due to fraud with intent to defeat or evade the fee imposed by this chapter, a penalty equal to the amount of said fee as determined by the Commission shall be paid by the purchaser in addition to said fee.

St.1983, c.669, s.13.

SECTION 14. (a) The Commission shall notify a purchaser by registered or certified mail of any failure to discharge in full the amount of the fee due under this Act and any penalty or interest assessed. The Commission shall grant a hearing on the matter of the imposition of said fee, or of any penalty or interest assessed, if a petition requesting such hearing is received by the Commission within thirty days after the mailing of said notice. The Commission shall notify the purchaser in writing by registered or certified mail of its determination concerning the deficiency, penalty or interest within fifteen days after said hearing. Any party aggrieved by a determination of the Commission concerning a deficiency, penalty or interest may, after payment of said deficiency, appeal to the district or superior court within three months after the mailing of notification of the determination of the Commission. Upon the failure to timely petition for a hearing, or appeal to said courts, within the time limits hereby established, the purchaser shall be bound by the terms of the notification, assessment or determination, as the case may be, and shall be barred from contesting the fee, and any interest and penalty, as determined by the Commission. All decisions of said courts shall be appealable. Every notice to be given under this section by the Commission shall be effective if mailed by certified or registered mail to the purchaser at the address stated in a recorded or registered instrument by virtue of which the purchaser holds any interest in land, the transfer of which gives rise to the fee which is the subject of such notice; and if no such address is stated or if such transfer is not evidenced by an instrument recorded or registered in the public records in Nantucket county, such notice shall be effective when so mailed to the purchaser in care of any person appearing of record to have a fee interest in such land, at the address of such person as set forth in an instrument recorded or registered in Nantucket county.

(b) All fees, penalties and interest required to be paid pursuant to this chapter shall constitute a personal debt of the purchaser and may be recovered in an action of contract or in any other appropriate action, suit or proceeding brought by the Commission; said action, suit or proceeding shall be subject to the provisions of chapter two hundred and sixty of the General Laws.

(c) If any purchaser liable to pay the fee established by this act neglects or refuses to pay the same, the amount, including any interest and penalty thereon, shall be a lien in favor of the Commission upon all property and rights to property, whether real or personal, belonging to such purchaser. Said lien shall arise at the time of transfer and shall continue until the liability for such amount is satisfied. Said lien shall in any event terminate not later than six years following the time of transfer. Said lien shall not be valid as against any mortgagee, pledgee, purchaser or judgment creditor unless notice thereof has been filed by the Commission (a) with respect to real property or fixtures, in the registry of deeds for Nantucket county, or (b) with respect to personal property, in the office in which a security or financing statement or notice with respect to the property would be filed in order to perfect a nonpossessory security interest belonging to the person named in the relevant notice, subject to the same limitations as set forth in section fifty of chapter sixty-two C of the General Laws.

In any case where there has been a refusal or neglect to pay any fee, interest or penalties imposed by this act, whether or not levy has been made, the commission, in addition to other modes of relief, may direct a civil action to be filed in a district or superior court of the commonwealth to enforce the lien of the Commission under this section with respect to such liability or to subject any property of whatever nature, of the delinquent, or in which he has any right, title or interest, to the payment of such liability.

The Commission may issue a waiver or release of any lien imposed by this section. Such waiver or release shall be conclusive evidence that the lien upon the property covered by the waiver or release is extinguished.

St.1983, c.669, s.14. Amended by St.1984, c.407, s.5

Historical Note

St.1984, c.407, s.5 amended subsection (c) of section 14 by inserting after the word "sixty-two" the letter: -C.

SECTION 14A. Upon termination or dissolution of the land bank, the title to all funds and other properties owned by it which remain after payment or the making of provision for payment of all bonds, notes and other obligations of the land bank shall vest in the town of Nantucket.

St.1984, c.407, s.4.

SECTION 14B. This act, being necessary for the welfare of the town and county of Nantucket and their inhabitants, shall be liberally construed to effect the purposes hereof.

St.1984, c.407, s.4.

SECTION 14C. The provisions of this act are severable, and if any provision hereof, including without limitation any exemption from the fee imposed hereby, shall be held invalid in any circumstances such invalidity shall not affect any other provisions or circumstances. This act shall be construed in all respects so as to meet all constitutional requirements. In carrying out the purposes and provisions of this act, all steps shall be taken which are necessary to meet constitutional requirements whether or not such steps are required by statute.

St.1984, c.407, s.4. Amended by St.1985, c.202, s.1.

Historical Note

St.1985, c.202, s.1 amended section 14C by inserting the words "including without limitation any exemption from the fee imposed hereby," in the first sentence.

SECTION 15. This act shall become effective upon its acceptance by vote of a town meeting of the town of Nantucket on February first, nineteen hundred and eighty-four.

St.1983, c.669, s.15.

St. 1983, c.669 approved December 20, 1983, effective February 1, 1984.
St. 1984, c.407 approved December 27, 1984, emergency letter January 3, 1984 9:42 a.m.
St.1985, c.202 approved July 29, 1985 1:15 p.m.
St.1987, c.666 approved January 6, 1988, effective February 5, 1988.

MARTHA'S VINEYARD LAND BANK

AN ACT ESTABLISHING THE DUKES COUNTY LAND BANK

Chapter 736 of the Acts of 1985
as amended by
Chapter 673 of the Acts of 1987

Be it enacted by the Senate and House of Representatives in General Court assembled, and by the authority of the same, as follows:

SECTION 1. For purposes of this act, the words and phrases set forth in this section shall have the following meanings:-

"Fund", shall refer to the Martha's Vineyard Land Bank Fund established under the provisions of section eight.

"Institutional lender", any bank as defined in section one of chapter one hundred and sixty-seven of the General Laws, any insurance company as defined in section one of chapter one hundred and seventy-five of the General Laws, and any mortgage company or investment company that made more than twenty mortgage loans in the calendar year preceding the year of the relevant mortgage for the purposes of subsection (m) of section twelve, and any national bank, federal savings and loan, federal savings bank, bank holding company, or state or federally chartered credit union.

"Land bank", the Martha's Vineyard Land Bank, established by section two.

"Land bank commission", the Martha's Vineyard land bank commission, established by section three.

"Legal representative", with respect to any person, shall mean any other person acting pursuant to a written power-of-attorney executed by such person; provided, however, that any affidavit attesting to the true and complete purchase price of real property, submitted to the land bank commission pursuant to section ten, may also be signed on behalf of such person by an attorney admitted to practice in the commonwealth.

"Purchaser", the transferee, grantee or recipient of any real property interests.

"Purchase price", all consideration paid or transferred by or on behalf of a purchaser to a seller or his nominee, or for his benefit, for the transfer of any real property interest, and shall include, but not be limited to, all cash or its equivalent so paid or transferred, all cash or other property paid or transferred by or on behalf of the purchaser to discharge or reduce any obligation of the seller; the principal amount of all notes or their equivalent, or other deferred payments, given or promised to be given by or on behalf of the purchaser to the seller or his nominee; the outstanding balance of all obligations of the seller which are assumed by the purchaser or to which the real property interest transferred remains subject after the transfer, determined at the time of transfer but excluding real estate taxes and other municipal liens or assessments which are not overdue at the time of transfer; and the fair market value at the time of transfer of any other consideration or thing of value paid or transferred by or on behalf of the purchaser, including, but not limited to, any property, goods or services paid, transferred or rendered in exchange for such real property interest.

"Real property interest", any present or future legal or equitable interest in or to real property, and any beneficial interest therein, including the interest of any beneficiary in a trust which holds any legal or equitable interest in real property, but shall not include any interest which is limited to any or all of the following: the dominant estate in any easement or right of way; the right to enforce any restriction; any estate at will or at sufferance, and any estate for years having a term of less than thirty years; the reversionary right, condition, or right of entry for condition broken; the interest of a mortgagee or other secured party in any mortgage or security agreement; and the interest of a stockholder in a corporation, or a partner in a partnership, unless any real property interest has been transferred to such corporation or partnership for the purpose of evading the fee imposed by section ten.

"Seller", the transferor, grantor or immediate former owner of any real property interests.

"Time of transfer", of any real property interest shall mean, the time at which such transfer is legally effective as between the parties thereto, and, in any event, with respect to a transfer evidenced by an instrument recorded with the appropriate registry of deeds or filed with the assistant recorder of the appropriate registry district, not later than the time of such recording or filing.

"Town advisory board", a town board created in each of the towns of Chilmark, Edgartown, Gay Head, Oak Bluffs, Tisbury, and West Tisbury to assist the land bank commission in administering this act, such advisory board to consist of one representative duly appointed, either from its membership or otherwise, by each of the following town boards should they exist: conservation commission, planning board, board of assessors, board of health, park and recreation commission, board of selectmen and water commission.

SECTION 2. There is hereby established a Martha's Vineyard land bank, to be administered by a land bank commission established by section three, for the purpose of acquiring and holding and managing land and interest in land of the types set forth in section five. The land bank is hereby constituted a body politic and corporate and a public instrumentality and the exercise of the powers herein conferred upon the land bank shall be deemed to be the performance of an essential governmental function.

This act shall not effect the eligibility of any member town to receive funds under the land conservation program created under section eleven of chapter one hundred and thirty-two A of the General Laws, or under any similar state program.

SECTION 3. The land bank shall be administered by a land bank commission, consisting of seven persons, of whom there shall be one person who is a legal resident of each of the towns of Chilmark, Edgartown, Gay Head, Oak Bluffs, Tisbury, and West Tisbury, each person to be elected for a three year term, in the same manner as other elected town officials, provided that the initial terms, drawn by lot by the initial six appointed members, shall be staggered so that two members are elected each year, following the initial election of members; and provided, further, that the county commissioners shall, respectively, appoint the initial six members, including one person who is a legal resident of each of the six towns that comprise the land bank to serve from the effective date of this act until the first elections of the regular members at each town's first regular or special town election following the effective date of this act. The secretary of environmental affairs or his designee shall be a voting member of the land bank commission. Members shall serve without compensation. The initial appointed members shall adopt temporary rules and regulations to the extent necessary to conduct business until the regular members are elected. The land bank commission shall elect a chairman and a vice chairman from among its regular members; shall elect a secretary and a treasurer who may be the same person, but who need not be members of the land bank commission; and shall adopt, after holding a public hearing and after requesting recommendations from the town advisory board of each of the six member towns that comprise the commission, rules and regulations for conducting its internal affairs and procedural guidelines for carrying out its responsibilities under this act. The land bank commission shall also adopt a management plan for managing each of its land holdings in a manner consistent with section five. In preparing a management plan for any parcel of land, the land bank commission shall use, as guidelines, the open space and master plans, if any, of the town or towns in which such parcel is located and shall request the recommendations of the town advisory board of such town or towns; and the adoption or change of any such management plan shall be subject tot he approval of at least two-thirds of the members of the town advisory board of each such town or towns. Decisions of the land bank commission shall be by majority vote of those present and voting at a meeting, and no business shall be transacted at any meeting unless a majority of the town representative members is present; provided that decisions to acquire interests in land and to request state approval of any proposed disposition of an interest in any parcel of land or of any change in its use shall require the affirmative vote of at least a majority of the town representative members of the land bank commission. The land bank commission shall keep accurate records of its meetings and actions and shall file an annual report which shall be distributed with the annual report of each member town.

SECTION 4. The land bank commission shall, subject to the provisions of this act, have the power and authority to: (a) acquire, by purchase or gift, fee simple interests, and any lesser interests, in any parcel of land situated within any of the towns that comprise the land bank commission, of the types set forth in section five, including any improvements thereon; provided, however, that the land bank commission shall, in considering any such acquisition, use as guidelines the open space and master plans, if any, of the town or towns in which such parcel is located, and provided further that any such acquisition shall require the approval of the town advisory board of any such town or towns; (b) accept gifts of funds to further the purposes of the land bank; (c) take any such interests in land by eminent domain pursuant to chapter seventy-nine of the General Laws, but only by a vote of the land bank commission in which at least a majority [of] town representative members vote in favor of such taking and further, only after having been authorized to do so in each instance by a two-thirds majority vote of each town that comprises the land bank commission at its annual or special town meeting, and further, only after first making a reasonable majority vote of each town that comprises the land bank commission at its annual or special town meeting, and further, only after first making a reasonable effort to negotiate the acquisition thereto by purchase; (d) dispose of all or any part of its interests in any parcel of land, or change the use of such parcel, but only with the approval of the town advisory board of the town or towns in which such parcel is located and with the approval of the secretary of environmental affairs and subject to the provisions of Article XCVII of the Articles of Amendment to the Constitution of the Commonwealth, to the extent applicable; (e) incur debt, pledging the full faith and credit of each of the towns that comprise the land bank commission but only after having been authorized to do so in each instance by a two-thirds majority town meeting vote of each town; and incur debt, without such town meeting authorization, by pledging the full faith and credit of the land bank commission; (f) prepare an annual budget, which shall be subject to approval by the town advisory boards of the majority of the member towns of the land bank commission; (g) hire such staff and obtain such professional services as are necessary in order to perform its duties; (h) administer and manage its interests in any parcel of land in a manner consistent with section five and with the land management plan adopted for such parcel under section three; (i) expend funds to supplement municipal, state, or federal funds for the purchase of interests in land of the types set forth in section five; and (j) adopt such regulations and procedures as it deems necessary or appropriate, subject to the provisions of this act, regarding the use and investment of its funds and the keeping of records and accounts.

SECTION 4A. Each member town is hereby authorized to appropriate money to be deposited in the fund as provided in section eight or to provide funds to repay notes of such member town issued pursuant to section four C and, when authorized by a two-thirds vote as defined in section one of chapter forty-four of the General Laws, to incur debt of such member town for such purposes in accordance with the provisions of clause (3) of section seven of said chapter forty-four.

SECTION 4B. The land bank is hereby empowered to issue its bonds and notes, including notes in anticipation of bonds, for the purpose of acquiring land and interests in land as provided in section four. The proceeds of such bonds or notes may be used to pay, in whole or in part, acquisition costs; to provide reserves for debt service and other expenses; to pay consulting, appraisal, advisory and legal fees and costs incidental to the issuance and sale of such bonds or notes; to purchase, refund or renew bonds or notes previously issued; and to pay any other costs and expenses of the land bank necessary for the accomplishment of its purposes. Bonds or notes issued under this act shall be authorized by the land bank commission which shall have full power and authority to determine the amount, form, terms, conditions, provisions for the payment of interest and all other details thereof and to provide for their sale and issuance at such price and in such manner as the land bank commission shall determine, subject only to any limitations set forth in this act. Unless each member town shall have authorized by a two-thirds vote of a town meeting the pledging of the full faith and credit of such towns to secure an issue of bonds or notes of the land bank, all bonds or notes issued hereunder shall be payable solely from the fees and other revenues of the land bank pledged to their payment and shall not be deemed a pledge of the full faith and credit of the any town in the county of Dukes County. Bonds and notes issued hereunder shall not be deemed a pledge of the full faith and credit of the county of Dukes County, the commonwealth or, except as provided in the preceding sentence in the case of the member towns, any political subdivision thereof or therein.

The land bank commission may enter into any agreements, including without limitation a loan agreement and a trust agreement, necessary to effectuate and to secure any bonds or notes issued by the land bank. Such agreements may pledge or assign, in whole or in part, the revenues and other money held or to be received by the land bank. Such agreements may contain provisions for protecting and enforcing the rights, security and remedies of the holders of such bonds or notes, including, without limiting the generality of the foregoing, provisions defining defaults and providing for remedies in the event thereof which may include the acceleration of maturities and covenants setting forth the duties of, and limitations on, the land bank in relation to the custody, safeguarding, investment and application of money, the issuance of additional debt obligations, the use of any surplus proceeds of the borrowing, including any investment earnings thereon, and the establishment of special funds and reserves.

The pledge of any such agreement shall be valid and binding and shall be deemed continuously perfected for the purposes of the Uniform Commercial Code from the time when the pledge is made; the revenues, money, rights and proceeds so pledged and then held or thereafter acquired or received by the land bank shall immediately be subject to the lien of such pledge without any physical delivery or segregation thereof or further act; and the lien of any such pledge shall be valid and binding against all parties having claims of any kind in tort, contract or otherwise against any member town or the county of Dukes County, irrespective of whether such parties have notice thereof. No document by which a pledge is created need be filed or recorded except in the records of the land bank and no filing need be made under the Uniform Commercial Code.

The trustee with respect to any such trust agreement entered into pursuant to this section shall be a trust company or a bank having the powers of a trust company within the commonwealth. Any such trust agreement may provide that any money received thereunder may be held, deposited or invested by the trustee, notwithstanding the provisions of section eight, pending the disbursement thereof, in any deposits or investments which are lawful for the funds of savings banks and shall provide that any officer with whom or any bank or trust company with which such money shall be deposited shall act as trustee of such money and shall hold and apply the same for the purposes hereof and thereof, subject to such regulation or limitation as this act or such trust agreement may provide.

It shall be lawful for any bank or trust company within the commonwealth to act as depository of the proceeds of bonds or notes, revenues or other money hereunder and to furnish such indemnifying bonds or to pledge such security, if any, as may be required by the land bank commission. Any trust agreement entered into pursuant to this section may set forth the rights and remedies of the holders of any bonds or notes and of the trustee and may restrict the individual right of action by any such holders. In addition to the foregoing, any such trust agreement may contain such other provisions as the land bank commission may deem reasonable and proper. All expenses incurred in carrying out the provisions of such trust agreement may be (i) treated as part of the cost of operation of the land bank and (ii) paid from the revenues or other funds pledged or assigned to the payment of the principal of and the premium, if any, and interest on the bonds or notes or from any other funds available to the land bank. In addition to other security provided herein or otherwise by law, bonds or notes issued under this section may be secured, in whole or in part, by insurance or by letters or lines of credit or other credit facilities issued to the land bank by any bank, trust company or other financial institution, within or without the commonwealth, and the land bank may pledge or assign any of its revenues as security for the reimbursement by the land bank to the issuers of such letters or lines of credit, insurance or credit facilities of any payments made thereunder. [100]

SECTION 4C. If at any time any principal or interest is due or about to come due on any bonds or notes of the land bank to secure which the full faith and credit of the member towns shall have been pledged and funds to pay the same are not available, the land bank commission shall certify to each town treasurer and the selectmen of each member town the amount required to meet such obligations and the town treasurers shall thereupon pay over to the land bank the amount so certified from any funds in the treasury. The amount certified to and payable by each member town shall be determined by applying to the aggregate amount so certified a fraction the numerator of which shall be the amount of revenue derived by the land bank from the fee imposed by section ten upon the transfer of real property interests in such town during the period from the commencement of operations of the land bank to and including the last day of the month preceding the month in which such certification is made, and the denominator of which shall be the total amount of revenue derived from such fee upon the transfer of real property interests during such period in all the member towns whose full faith and credit has been pledged to secure such obligations. For the purpose of providing or restoring to the treasury the sums so paid over to the land bank, each town treasurer, with the approval of the selectmen, is authorized to incur debt outside the town's debt limit and issue notes therefor for a period not exceeding two years and to renew or refund the same from time to time until the town shall have received from the land bank sufficient funds to repay such notes and the interest thereon in full. Whenever the towns shall have been required to pay over any sums of money to the land bank under this section, the land bank shall be precluded from acquiring any additional property, or issuing any of its bonds or notes for purposes other than repaying the towns, until the land bank shall have repaid the towns in full for all sums paid to the land bank hereunder, including interest on any notes issued for such purpose, unless the towns shall have appropriated sufficient funds for such purpose at a town meeting or meetings.

SECTION 4D. Bonds and notes issued under the provisions of this act are hereby made securities in which all public officers and public bodies of the commonwealth and its political subdivisions, all insurance companies, trust companies in their commercial departments, savings banks, cooperative banks, banking associations, investment companies, executors, administrators, trustees and other fiduciaries may properly and legally invest funds, including capital in their control or belonging to them. Such bonds and notes are hereby made securities which may properly and legally be deposited with and received by any state or municipal officer or any agency or political subdivision of the commonwealth for any purpose for which the deposit of bonds or obligations of the commonwealth is now or may hereafter be authorized by law.

SECTION 4E. Notwithstanding any of the provisions of this act or any recitals in any bonds or notes issued under this act, all such bonds and notes shall be deemed to be investment securities under the Uniform Commercial Code.

SECTION 4F. Bonds and notes may be issued under this act without obtaining the consent of any department, division, commission, board, bureau or agency of any member town or of the county of Dukes County, except that the full faith and credit of any member town shall not be pledged for the payment of such bonds or notes unless such pledge shall have been authorized by the appropriate two-thirds vote or votes as provided in section four, and without any other proceedings or the happening of any other conditions or things that those proceedings, conditions or things which are specifically required therefor by this act. The validity of and security for any bonds and notes issued by the land bank shall not be affected by the existence or non-existence of any such consent or other proceedings, conditions or things.

SECTION 4G. The land bank and all its revenues, income and real and personal property used solely by the land bank in furtherance of its public purposes shall be exempt from taxation and from betterments and special assessments and the land bank shall not be required to pay any tax, excise or assessment to or for the commonwealth or any of its political subdivisions. Bonds and notes issued by the land bank, their transfer and the income therefrom, including any profit made on the sale thereof, shall at all times be exempt from taxation within the commonwealth. The provisions of section twenty-seven C of chapter twenty-nine of the General Laws shall not apply to this section or any other provision of this chapter.

SECTION 5. Interests in land to be acquired shall be situated in a member town and may consist of any of the following: (a) land to protect existing and future well fields, aquifers and recharge areas; (b) agricultural lands; (c) forest land; (d) fresh and salt water marshes and other wetlands; (e) ocean and pond frontage, beaches, dunes, and adjoining backlands, to protect their natural and scenic resources; (f) land to protect scenic vistas; (g) land for nature or wildlife preserve; (h) easements for trails and for publicly owned lands; and (i) land for passive recreational use.

SECTION 6. The land bank commission shall retain any real property interest acquired pursuant to this act predominantly in its natural, scenic or open condition, and shall not restrict access to any property interest on the basis of residency or domicile. Notwithstanding the foregoing, the land bank commission may make improvements to any land held for passive recreational use that are not inconsistent with such use. With respect to any such real property interest, the land bank commission shall not permit any of the following without the approval of the town advisory board of the town or towns in which such real property is located and without the approval of the secretary of environmental affairs: (a) construction or placing of buildings, roads, signs, billboards, or other advertising utilities or other structures on or above the surface, (b) dumping of placing of soil or other substance or material as landfill, or dumping or placing of trash, waste or unsightly or offensive materials, (c) removal or destruction of trees, shrubs, or other vegetation, (d) excavation, dredging, or removal of loam, peat, gravel, soil, rock, or other mineral substance in such manner as to affect the surface, (e) surface use except for purposes permitting the land or water area to remain predominantly in its natural condition, (f) activities detrimental to drainage, flood control, water conservation, erosion control, or soil conservation, or (g) other acts or uses detrimental to such retention of land or water areas. In determining whether or not to approve a request from the land bank commission to use or improve any real property interest acquired by the land bank commission in a manner otherwise prohibited by this section, the secretary of environmental affairs shall consider whether such request is in the interest of conservation and any national, state, regional or local program in furtherance thereof, and also any public, state, regional or local comprehensive land use or development plan affecting the land, and any known proposal by a governmental body for use of the land.

SECTION 7. The land bank commission shall file annually with the secretary of environmental affairs a report of its activities during the year preceding such filing. The report shall list all real property interests currently held by the land bank commission, including a description of the use thereof, and shall include all acquisitions, improvements and dispositions of real property interests by the land bank commission during such year. The report shall also include a current plan for its future operations which shall be, as far as possible, consistent with the open space and master plans of each of the towns and with any regional planning in the area. The secretary of environmental affairs may require any other information which said secretary deems important.

SECTION 8. The land bank commission shall meet its financial obligations by drawing upon a fund, to be set up as a revolving or sinking account within the treasury of the county of Dukes County. Deposits into the fund shall include (a) funds appropriated, borrowed, or transferred to be deposited into the fund by vote of the county commissioners of the county of Dukes County or of town meetings of the towns that comprise the land bank commission; (b) voluntary contributions of money and other liquid assets to the fund; (c) revenues from fees imposed upon the transfer of real property interests as set forth in section ten occurring after the effective date of this act as set forth in section fifteen, together with payments of interest and penalties under section thirteen; and (d) proceeds from disposal of real property or interests. Grants or gifts of money or other assets to the land bank shall be expended only for the purpose of the grant or gift and subject to any restrictions or limitations imposed thereon by the grantor or donor thereof. All expenses lawfully incurred by the land bank commission in carrying out the provisions of this act shall be evidenced by proper vouchers and shall be paid by the county treasurer of said county only upon submission of warrants duly approved by the land bank commission. The county treasurer of said county shall prudently invest available assets of the fund in accordance with the regulations and procedures adopted by the land bank commission pursuant to clause (j) of section four, and all income thereon shall accrue to the fund.

SECTION 8A. An account shall be established by the land bank commission for each member town of the land bank. The county treasurer shall administer all transactions for the individual town accounts. Of the revenues collected under this act, fifty per cent shall remain in the fund, to be directly administered by the land bank commission in accordance with the provisions of this act. The remaining fifty per cent of the revenues collected shall be transferred to the individual town accounts in proportion to the amount of collected land bank revenues derived from transfer of any real property interest in any real property within each respective town. Money in the individual town account of each member town may be expended by the land bank commission, subject to the approval of at least a majority of the members of the town advisory board of such town, for the purchase of land or interests in land permitted by this act. Within or outside the borders of such town, or for any other purpose permitted by this act, including the payment of debt service on bonds or notes issued by the land bank hereunder. With the approval of at least two-thirds of the members of the town advisory board of any member town, an agreement entered into under section four B may pledge or assign in whole or in part, the revenues held in, or to be received for the account of, the individual town account of such town to secure any bonds or notes issued by the land bank for a purpose so approved by the town advisory board.

SECTION 9. The land bank commission shall keep a full and accurate account of its actions including a record as to when, from or to whom, and on what account money has been paid or received relative to this act, and as to when, from and to whom and for what consideration real property interests have been acquired, improved, or disposed of. Said records or accounts shall be subject to examination by the director of accounts or his agent pursuant to section forty-five of chapter thirty-five of the General Laws.

Said county treasurer shall keep a full and accurate account stating when, from or to whom, and on what account money has been paid or received relative to the activities of the land bank commission and the land bank. Said account shall be subject to examination by the director of accounts or his agent pursuant to section forty-four of chapter thirty-five of the General Laws.

SECTION 10. There is hereby imposed a fee equal to two per cent of the purchase price upon the transfer of any real property interest in any real property situated in a member town or towns. The fee percentage may be reduced by a two-thirds vote in favor of such reduction at the annual town meetings of a majority of the member towns in a single calendar year; provided, however, that no reduction in the fee percentage shall take effect until all bonds and notes of the land bank issued prior thereto pursuant to section four B shall have been paid in full. Said fee shall be the liability of the purchaser of such real property interest, and any agreement between the purchaser and the seller or any other person with reference to the allocation of the responsibility for bearing said fee shall not affect such liability of the purchaser. Such fee shall be paid to the land bank commission or its designee, and shall be accompanied by a copy of the deed or other instrument evidencing such transfer, if any, and an affidavit signed under oath or under the pains and penalties of perjury by the purchaser or his legal representative, attesting to the true and complete purchase price and the basis, if any, upon which the transfer is claimed to be exempt in whole or in part from the fee imposed hereby. The land bank commission, or its designee, shall promptly thereafter execute and issue a certificate indicating that the appropriate fee has been paid or that the transfer is exempt from the fee, stating the basis for the exemption. The register of deeds for the county of Dukes County, and the assistant recorder for the registry district of the county of Dukes County, shall not record or register, or receive or accept for recording or registration, any deed, except a mortgage deed, relative to a real property interest in land situated in any town that is a member of the land bank commission to which has not been affixed such a certificate, executed by the land bank commission or its designee. Failure to comply with this requirement shall not affect the validity of any instrument. The land bank commission shall deposit all fees received hereunder with the county treasurer of the county of Dukes County as a part of the fund established by section eight. The fee imposed hereunder shall be due simultaneously with the time of transfer upon which it is imposed.

SECTION 11. At any time within seven days following the issuance of the certificate of payment of the fee imposed by section ten, the purchaser or his legal representative may return said certificate to the land bank commission or its designee for cancellation, together with an affidavit signed under oath or under the pains and penalties of perjury that the transfer, with respect to which such certificate was issued, has not been consummated, and thereupon the fee paid with respect to such transfer shall be forthwith returned to the purchaser or his legal representative.

SECTION 12. The following transfer of real property interests shall be exempt from the fee established by section ten. Except as otherwise provided, the purchaser shall have the burden of proof that any transfer is exempt hereunder:

(a) transfers to the government of the United States, the commonwealth, and any of their instrumentalities, agencies, or subdivisions;

(b) transfers which, without additional consideration, confirm, correct, modify or supplement a transfer previously made;

(c) transfers made as gifts without consideration; in any proceedings to determine the amount of any fee due hereunder, it shall be presumed that any transfer for consideration of less than fair market value of the real property interests transferred was made as a gift without consideration to the extent of the difference between the fair market value of the real property interests transferred and the amount of consideration claimed by the purchaser to have been paid or transferred, if the purchaser shall have been at the time of transfer the spouse, the lineal descendent, or the lineal ancestor of the seller, by blood or adoption, and otherwise it shall be presumed that consideration was paid in an amount equal to the fair market value of the real property interests transferred, at the time of transfer;

(d) transfer to the trustees of a trust in exchange for a beneficial interest received by the seller in such trust; distributions by the trustees of a trust to the beneficiaries of such trust;

(e) transfers by operation of law without actual consideration, including but not limited to transfers occurring by virtue of the death or bankruptcy of the owner of a real property interest;

(f) transfers made in partition of land and improvements thereto, under the provisions of chapter two hundred and forty-one of the General Laws;

(g) transfers to any charitable organization as defined in clause third of section five of chapter fifty-nine of the General Laws, or any religious organization, provided that the real property interests so transferred shall be held by the charitable or religious organization solely for its public, charitable or religious purposes;

(h) transfers to a mortgagee in foreclosure of the mortgage held by such mortgagee, and transfers of the property subject to a mortgage to the mortgagee in consideration of the forbearance of the mortgagee from foreclosing said mortgage;

(i) transfers made to a corporation or partnership at the time of its formation, pursuant to which transfer no gain or loss is recognized under the provisions of section three hundred and fifty-one of the Internal Revenue Code of 1954;

(j) transfers made to a stockholder of a corporation in liquidation of the corporation, and transfers made to a partner of a partnership in dissolution of the partnership;

(k) transfer consisting of the division of marital assets under the provisions of section thirty-four of chapter two hundred and eight of the General Laws or other provisions of law;

(l) transfers of property consisting in part of real property interests situated within a town that is a member of the land bank commission and in part of other property interests, to the extent that the property transferred consists of property other than real property situated within a town that is a member of the land bank commission provided that the purchaser shall furnish the land bank commission with such information as it shall require or request in support of the claim of exemption and manner of allocation of the consideration for such transfers; and

(m) the first one hundred thousand dollars of the purchase price of a transfer made to a natural person who, or whose spouse, at the time of such transfer has at no time owned or possessed any real property interest as defined in section one either within or without any member town, provided that such person makes the real property interest which is the subject of the transfer his or her actual domicile within two years of the time of transfer; provided, further, that in the event of a subsequent transfer within five years of the transfer exempted from the fee under this subsection, other than the transfer of a mortgage to an institutional lender, the fee exempted shall become due, together with accumulated interest and penalties, and in addition to any fee otherwise due as a result of the subsequent transfer. The purchaser shall certify as to the foregoing, and the land bank commission shall attach to the deed a certificate which shall recite the fact that there is running with the land a lien equal to the amount of the fee exempted plus accumulated interest and penalties until such time as all conditions of this subsection have been met. The land bank commission shall have the power, at any time and from time to time, to require any purchaser claiming the exempting provided by this subsection to furnish such evidence of compliance with the requirements of this subsection as the land bank commission shall deem necessary or appropriate. If any requirement or condition of this subsection is not met within the time specified, the amount of the fee exempted plus accumulated interest and penalties shall automatically become due and payable.

SECTION 13. A purchaser who fails to pay all or any portion of the fee established by section ten on or before the time when the same is due shall be liable for the following additional payments in addition to said fee:

(a) Interest. The purchaser shall pay interest on the unpaid amount of the fee to be calculated from the time of transfer at a rate equal to fourteen per cent per annum.

(b) Penalties. Any person who, without fraud or willful intent to defeat or evade a fee imposed by this act, fails to pay all or a portion of the fee within thirty days after the time of transfer, shall pay a penalty equal to five per cent of the outstanding fee as determined by the land bank commission for each month or portion thereof thereafter that the fee is not paid in full; provided, however, that in no event shall the amount of any penalty imposed hereunder exceed twenty-five per cent of the unpaid fee due at the time of transfer. Whenever the land bank commission determines that all or a portion of a fee due under this chapter was unpaid due to fraud with intent to defeat or evade the fee imposed by this chapter, a penalty equal to the amount of said fee as determined by the land bank commission shall be paid by the purchaser in addition to said fee.

SECTION 14. (a) The land bank commission shall notify a purchaser by registered or certified mail of any failure to discharge in full the amount of the fee due under this act and any penalty or interest assessed. The land bank commission shall grant a hearing on the matter of the imposition of said fee, or of any penalty or interest assessed, if a petition requesting such hearing is received by the land bank commission within thirty days after the mailing of said notice. The land bank commission shall notify the purchaser in writing by registered or certified mail of its determination concerning the deficiency, penalty or interest within fifteen days after said hearing. Any party aggrieved by a determination of the land bank commission concerning a deficiency, penalty or interest may, after payment of said deficiency, appeal to the district or superior court within three months after the mailing of notification of the land bank commission. Upon the failure to timely petition for a hearing, or appeal to said courts, within the time limits hereby established, the purchaser shall be bound by the terms of the notification, assessment or determination, as the case may be, and shall be barred from contesting the fee, and any interest and penalty, as determined by the land bank commission. All decisions of said courts shall be appealable. Every notice to be given under this section by the land bank commission shall be effective if mailed by certified or registered mail to the purchaser at the address stated in a recorded or registered instrument by virtue of which the purchaser holds any interest in land, the transfer of which gives rise to the fee which is the subject of such notice; and if no such address is stated or if such transfer is not evidenced by an instrument recorded or registered in the public records in the county of Dukes County, such notice shall be effective when so mailed to the purchaser in care of any person appearing of record to have a fee interest in such land, at the address of such person as set forth in an instrument recorded or registered in the county of Dukes County.

(b) All fees, penalties and interest required to be paid pursuant to this act shall constitute a personal debt of the purchaser and may be recovered in an action of contract or in any other appropriate action, suit or proceeding brought by the land bank commission; said action, suit or proceedings shall be subject to the provisions of chapter two hundred and sixty of the General Laws.

(c) If any purchaser liable to pay the fee established by this act neglects or refuses to pay the same, the amount, including any interest and penalty thereon, shall be a lien in favor of the land bank commission upon all property and rights to property, whether real or personal, belonging to such purchaser. Said lien shall arise at the time of transfer and shall continue until the liability for such amount is satisfied. Said lien shall in any event terminate not later than six years following the time of transfer. Said lien shall not be valid as against any mortgagee, pledge, purchaser or judgment creditor unless notice thereof has been filed by the land bank commission (i) with respect to real property or fixtures, in the registry of deeds for the county of Dukes County, or (ii) with respect to personal property, in the office in which a security or financing statement or notice with respect to the property would be filed in order to perfect a nonpossessory security interest belonging to the person named in the relevant notice, subject to the same limitation as set forth in section fifty of chapter sixty-two of the General Laws.

In any case where there has been a refusal or neglect to pay any fee, interest or penalties imposed by this act, whether or not levy has been made, the land bank commission, in addition to other modes of relief, may direct a civil action to be filed in a district or superior court of the commonwealth to enforce the lien of the land bank commission under this section with respect to such liability or to subject any property of whatever nature, of the delinquent, or in which he has any right, title or interest, to the payment of such liability.

The land bank commission may issue a waiver or release of any lien imposed by this section with the approval of the town advisory board of the town or towns in which the property subject to the lien is located. Such waiver or release shall be conclusive evidence that the lien upon the property covered by the waiver or release is extinguished.

SECTION 14A. This act, being necessary for the welfare of the member towns and the county of Dukes County and their inhabitants, shall be liberally construed to effect the purpose hereof.

SECTION 15. Any town that is a member of the land bank may withdraw therefrom by the affirmative vote of a majority of the voters at any regular or special town election; provided, however, that any real property interest held by the land bank and situated in a town that withdraws from the land bank shall continue to be held by the land bank until such time as the land bank is dissolved in accordanse with this act; provided, further, that no town may withdraw from the land bank until payment in full of all bonds and notes issued by the land bank prior to receipt by the land bank commission of written notice that an election has been called by such town to vote upon the question of such withdrawal. Any town that withdraws from the land bank shall not be liable for debts and obligations incurred by the land bank subsequent to receipt of such notice by the land bank commission. A town that has so withdrawn may renew its membership by the affirmative vote of a majority of the voters at any regular or special town election at which the question of acceptance has been placed on the ballot. Upon the withdrawal of a town from the land bank, all funds then held in the account established for such town pursuant to section eight A, after payment or provision for payment has been made in full on all bonds and notes issued by the land bank prior to receipt by the land bank commission of written notice that an election has been called by such town to vote upon the question of such withdrawal, shall be transferred to the fund established by section eight.

If the member towns in the land bank are reduced to a number less than three the land bank shall be dissolved; provided, however, that the fee imposed by section ten shall continue to be imposed in each member town until all bonds and notes of the land bank issued while such town was a member have been paid in full, and the land bank shall continue in existence during such time for the sole purpose of administering and collecting such fee. Upon dissolution of the land bank, title to all funds and other properties held by the land bank shall vest in the towns of the county of Dukes County as herein provided after provision is made for payment of all bonds, notes and other obligations of the land bank. Interests in land held by the land bank at the time of dissolution shall be transferred to the town or towns in which the land is situated, and placed under the control and management of the local conservation commission who shall maintain, protect, limit the future use of, improve, or otherwise conserve and properly utilize open spaces of land. Such land shall remain subject to the provisions of Article XCVII of the Articles of Amendments to the Constitution of the Commonwealth. Funds held by the land bank shall be transferred to the towns of the county of Dukes County as hereinafter provided, to be held in trust for the purpose of holding and managing the land transferred to the towns pursuant to this paragraph and other land held under the control and management of the local conservation commissions of the towns. Funds shall be transferred to each town in proportion to the fees generated by lands situated within such town over the life of the land bank under this act.

The land bank commission shall submit no amendment of this act to the general court unless and until such amendment has been approved by two-thirds of the member towns by the affirmative vote of a majority of the voters of the town at any regular or special election.

SECTION 16. Acceptance of this act, by each of the towns of Chilmark, Edgartown, Gay Head, Oak Bluffs, Tisbury, and West Tisbury shall be by the affirmative vote of a majority of the voters at any regular or special town election at which the question of acceptance has been placed on the ballot. This act shall become effective on the date on which acceptance by all of said towns has been effected.
NOTE: Section 20 of Chapter 673 of the Acts of 1987, entitled "AN ACT FURTHER REGULATING THE MARTHA'S VINEYARD LAND BANK" provides as follows:

SECTION 20. This act shall take effect upon its passage, or upon its approval by two-thirds of the member towns by the affirmative vote of a majority of the voters of such towns at any annual or special town meeting, whichever is the last to occur; provided that such approval may take place either before or after the passage of this act.

DL340

A-3

85 -- S954

STATE OF RHODE ISLAND

IN GENERAL ASSEMBLY

JANUARY SESSION, A.D. 1985

AN ACT

ESTABLISHING THE LITTLE COMPTON
AGRICULTURAL CONSERVANCY TRUST

<u>Introduced By</u>: Senator Forte

<u>Date Introduced</u>: April 24, 1985

<u>Referred To</u>: Read and Passed

It is enacted by the General Assembly as follows:

<u>Section 1.</u> There is hereby established a Little Compton Agricultural Conservancy Trust (hereinafter called Trust) for the primary purpose of acquiring development rights to agricultural property within the town. The Trust shall have as a secondary purpose the acquisition of agricultural property, and/or other property, or interest therein, to preserve open spaces, fresh and saltwater marshes, estuaries and adjoining uplands, groundwater recharging areas, land providing access to the ocean, land for bicycle paths and land for future public recreational facilities and use.

<u>Section 2.</u> The Trust shall be administered by seven (7) trustees, five (5) of whom shall be appointed by the town coucil with at least one (1) being an active farmer. The trustees who are first appointed shall be designated to serve for terms of one (1), two (2), three (3), four (4), and five (5) years respectively. Thereafter

trustees shall be appointed as aforesaid for a term of office of five (5) years, except that all vacancies occurring during a term shall be filled for the unexpired term. In addition to the five (5) trustees appointed by the town council, the current chairperson, or member designee, of the Little Compton Conservation Commission and Little Compton Planning Board shall also be trustees.

Trustees shall be resident electors of the town of Little Compton, shall serve without compensation and shall hold office until their successors have been appointed. No trustee may be an elected officer or salaried employee of the town.

Section 3. The members of the Trust shall elect a chairperson, vice-chairperson, and treasurer from amongst its members. The trustees shall elect or appoint a secretary who need not be a voting member of the Trust. The term of office of the office of the chairperson, vice-chairperson, treasurer and secretary, unless otherwise prescribed by the Little Compton town council, shall be for the calendar year, or for that portion therefor remaining after each such officer is designated or elected.

Section 4. The trustees may adopt reasonable rules and regulations governing the conduct of Trust affairs, including the acquisition and management of its holdings not inconsistent with the provisions of this act. All rules and regulations of the Trust are subject to the approval of the town council. Decisions of the trustees shall be by majority vote of those present and voting, and no business shall be transacted without four (4) members present. The trustees shall keep accurate records of their meetings and actions and shall file an annual report which shall be printed in the annual town report. All meetings of the Trust shall be open to the public.

Section 5. The Trust shall have the authority to acquire any real property from consenting land owner(s), situated in Little Compton, or any interest therein, which it shall deem important to preserve or maintain in an open or agricultural condition. With the exception of property acquired for public recreation purposes, such property shall be held by the Trust subject to the condition that it shall be used for open space or agricultural use. The trustees shall afford priority to the acquisition of development rights of agricultural lands.

<u>Section 6.</u> The Trust shall also have power to:

a. Purchase, receive by gift, or otherwise acquire real property and development rights, as defined in section 42-82-2 of the general laws or any interest in real property consistent with purposes of this Act;

b. Accept gifts, grants or loans of funds or services from any source, public or private, and comply, subject to the provisions of this Act, with any terms and conditions thereof;

c. Accept from state and/or federal agencies, loans or grants for use in carrying out its purposes and enter into agreements with such agencies respecting any such loans or grants;

d. Employ counsel, auditors, engineers, appraisers, private consultants, advisors, secretaries or other personnel needed to provide necessary services;

e. Administer and manage land and interests in land held by it in a manner which allows public use and/or enjoyment consistent with the natural and scenic resources thereof;

f. Otherwise do all things necessary for the performance of its duties, the fulfillment of its obligation and the conduct of its business.

<u>Section 7.</u> The electors of the town of Little Compton are hereby authorized to levy an additional tax upon real property transfers within said town in accordance with section 8 of this act. Said tax shall be levied at the annual financial town meeting and shall become effective on the first day of the next town fiscal year. The tax, once adopted, shall remain in effect unless the electors, when legally assembled, repeal said tax. The electors, when legally assembled, may also amend the rate of said tax.

Section 8. Whenever a tax is assessed by section 44-25-1 of the general laws on the transfer of real property situated in Little Compton, there is hereby imposed, in addition to said tax, an additional tax not to exceed the amount of five (5%) percent of that amount of the purchase price which exceeds seventy five thousand ($75,000) dollars.

In the case of real property which is situated in both Little Compton and Tiverton, Rhode Island or Westport, Massachusetts, the additional tax shall be imposed on that portion of the sales price, in relation to what the current assessed values, as determined by the Little Compton tax assessors and their counterpart in the abutting town, bear to the total sales price.

The payment of the additional tax hereby imposed shall be evidenced by the affixing of documentary stamps, provided by the Little Compton town clerk's office, to every original instrument presented for recording in the same manner as set forth in section 44-25-3 of said general laws. Said tax shall be the obligation of the buyer of real property unless otherwise agreed to by the parties to the transfer.

Section 9. All funds collected by virtue of said assessment shall be deposited in a fund to be set up as a revolving account by the treasurer of the town of Little Compton. Additional monies or other liquid assets received as voluntary contributions, grants or loans shall be deposited into said account.

Section 10. If any of the provisions of this act or if any rule, regulation or order thereunder or the application of such provision to any person or circumstances shall be held invalid, the remainder of this act and the application of this act or such rule, regulation or order to any person or circumstances, other than those as to which it is held invalid, shall not be affected thereby.

Section 11. This section shall take effect upon passage of the act. The remainder of this act shall take effect upon its approval by a majority of those voting to approve the act at an annual financial town meeting of the town of Little Compton.

=====
DL340
=====

S. 0954 H.

PUBLIC LAWS
CHAPTER
85-16

AN ACT

ESTABLISHING THE LITTLE COMPTON AGRICULTURAL CONSERVANCY TRUST

JT. COMM LEGISLATIVE AFFAIRS
LAW REVISION OFFICE

Presented by

IN THE SENATE APR 24 1985
on roll call vote
32 Ayes — 0 Nays
Read and PASSED Reading Clerk

APR 30 1985

APPROVED
MAY 03 1985
GOVERNOR

STATE OF RHODE ISLAND

IN GENERAL ASSEMBLY

JANUARY SESSION, A.D. 1986

AN ACT

RELATING TO THE PRESERVATION OF FARM LAND AND OPEN SPACE IN THE TOWN OF NEW SHOREHAM AND ESTABLISHING A LAND TRUST

(As Amended in 1987)

Introduced By: Senators Cecarelli, Forte, Coldberg, Farnum, Hanson et al

Date Introduced: January 15, 1986

Referred To: Senate Corporations

It is enacted by the General Assembly as follows:

SECTION 1. There is hereby established the Block Island land trust (hereinafter called the trust), a body politic and corporate and a public instrumentality. The trust shall have the authority to acquire, hold, and manage real property and interests therein situated in the town of New Shoreham consisting of open, agricultural, or littoral property, including existing and future wellfields and aquifer recharge areas, fresh and saltwater marshes and adjoining uplands, barrier beaches, wildlife habitats, land providing access to or views of the ocean, harbors, and ponds, land for bicycling and hiking paths and for future public recreational use, and land for agricultural use. With the exception of property acquired for public recreational purposes, the trust shall hold all property solely as open space or for agricultural uses or for water purposes as the trustees may determine.

SECTION 2. The trust shall be administered by five (5) trustees elected for staggered four (4) year terms, provided that the town council of the town of New Shoreham (hereinafter called the town council) shall appoint the initial five (5) persons to serve until the first regular town election following the acceptance of this act. At such first regular election there shall be elected two (2) trustees to serve for a term of two (2) years and three (3) trustees to serve for a term of four (4) years. Biennially thereafter at the regular town election, trustees shall be elected each for a term of four (4) years to succeed each trustee whose term has expired. Any vacancy occurring during a term shall be filled by appointment by the town council until the next regular town election, when such vacancy shall be filled for the unexpired term thereof. Trustees shall be electors of the town of New Shoreham, shall serve without compensation, and shall hold office until their successors have been named.

SECTION 3. The trustees of the trust shall elect a chairperson, vice-chairperson, and treasurer from among its members. The trustees shall elect or appoint a secretary who need not be a voting member of the trust. The term of office of the chairperson, vice-chairperson, treasurer and secretary, unless otherwise prescribed by the town council, shall be for one (1) year.

SECTION 4. The trustees may adopt reasonable rules and regulations governing the conduct of trust affairs, including the acquisition and management of its holdings, not inconsistent with the provisions of this act. All rules and regulations of the trust are subject to the approval of the town council. Decisions of the trustees shall be by majority vote of those present and voting, and no business shall be transacted without three (3) members present. The trustees shall keep accurate records of their meetings and actions and shall file an annual report which shall be printed in the annual town report. All meetings of the trust shall be open to the public in accordance with chapter 46 of title 42 of the general laws.

SECTION 5. The trust shall have the power to: a. Purchase, receive by gift, or otherwise acquire fee simple or lesser interests in real property, including development rights as defined in section 42-82-2 of the general laws, or any interest in real property consistent with purposes of this act;

b. Accept gifts, grants or loans of funds or services from any source, public or private, and comply, subject to the provisions of this act, with any terms and conditions thereof;

c. Accept from state and/or federal agencies, loans or grants for use in carrying out the trust's purposes and enter into agreements with such agencies respecting any such loans or grants;

d. Employ counsel, auditors, engineers, appraisers, private consultants, advisors, secretaries or other personnel needed to perform its duties;

e. Administer and manage land and interests in land held by it in a manner which allows public use and enjoyment consistent with the natural and scenic resources thereof, including conveyance of any such land or interests in land to, and contracts with, nonprofit organizations, provided such land shall continue to be used in a manner consistent with the purposes of this act and with the terms of any grant or devise by which such land was acquired by the trust;

f. Incur debt, only after authorization in each instance by vote of a financial town meeting of the town of New Shoreham in accordance with section 12 of this act. The trust shall be obligated to pay debt service on all such debt to the extent funds are available and to reimburse the town for any town funds expended to pay such debt service. Whenever the town of New Shoreham shall have been required to pay over any sums of money to the trust, the trust shall be precluded from acquiring any additional property until the trust shall have repaid the town of New Shoreham in full for all sums paid to the trust hereunder and to reimburse the town for any town funds expended to pay such debt service.

[132]

g. Dispose of all or any portion of its real property or interests therein held by it, whenever in the opinion of the trustees said lands or properties have become unsuitable or have ceased to be used for the purposes set forth in this act. Such disposition shall be made only by a vote of the trustees in which at least four (4) members vote in favor of such a disposition and further only after having been approved by a two thirds (2/3) vote of an annual or special financial town meeting of the town of New Shoreham. Nothing in this subsection shall be construed to authorize the sale, lease or conveyance of lands or improvements held by the trust as part of a charitable trust or acquired by gift or devise for the public use, whether or not such gift or devise is subject to a condition subsequent or reverter.

h. Otherwise do all things necessary for the performance of its duties, the fulfillment of its obligation and the conduct of its business.

Section 6. The electors of the town of New Shoreham are hereby authorized to levy a fee not to exceed five percent (5%) of the amount of the purchase price upon real property transfers within said town in accordance with section 7 of this act. The amount of said fee shall be adopted at an annual or special financial town meeting and shall become effective on the first day of the next month which occurs at least thirty (30) days after the vote adopting the fee. The fee, once adopted, shall remain in effect unless the electors at an annual or special financial town meeting amend the rate of or repeal said fee. Said fee shall not be changed or repealed without notice of the proposed change or repeal having been placed on the warrant for a financial town meeting.

For the purposes of this chapter "purchase price" shall mean all consideration paid or transferred by or on behalf of a buyer to a seller or his nominee or for his benefit for the transfer of any real property interests, and shall include, but not be limited to, all cash or its equivalent so paid or transferred; all cash or other property paid or transferred by or on behalf of the buyer to discharge or reduce any obligation of the seller; the principal amount of all notes or their equivalent, or other deferred payments, given or promised to be given by or on behalf of the buyer to the seller or his nominee; the outstanding balance of all obligations of the seller which are assumed by the buyer or to which the real property interests transferred remain subject after the transfer, determined at the time of transfer, but excluding real estate taxes and other municipal liens or assessments which are not overdue at the time of transfer; and the fair market value, at the time of transfer, of any other consideration or thing of value paid or transferred by or on behalf of the purchaser, including, but not limited to, any property, goods or services paid, transferred or rendered in exchange for such real property interests.

Section 7. Whenever there is a transfer of real property situated in the town of New Shoreham on which there is imposed a tax under section 44-25-1 of the general laws, there is hereby imposed, in addition to said tax, a fee not to exceed the amount of five percent (5%) of the amount of the purchase price as adopted pursuant to section 6. The payment of the fee hereby imposed shall be made to the trust and shall be evidenced by a certificate, provided by the trust or its designee, indicating the fee has been paid or that the transfer is exempt from the fee, and stating the basis for the exemption. Said certificate shall be entered upon the land records at the same time of the recording of the land transfer to which it refers. The town clerk shall not record or register, or receive or accept for recording or registration, any deed, except a mortgage deed, to which has not been affixed such certificate, executed by the trust or its designee. Failure to comply with this requirement shall not affect the validity of any instrument. Said fee shall be the obligation of the buyer of real property. Any agreement between the buyer and the seller or any other person with reference to the allocation of the responsibility for bearing such fee shall not affect such liability of the buyer. [134]

Notwithstanding the foregoing, whenever there is a conveyance of real property interests and a conveyance of personalty related thereto at or about the same time, the allocations of payments between real estate and personalty agreed to by the buyer and seller shall not determine the amount of the fee due pursuant to this section; instead, the trust may require payment of the fee referred to in this section based upon the then fair market value of the real property interests so conveyed as determined by the trust.

The fee authorized by this section and by section 6 shall also be imposed on the fair market value of real property interests held in the name of or otherwise owned by: (1) a corporation, when there is a transfer by the controlling stockholders of their interest in the stock of the corporation; and (2) a partnership, when there is a change in composition of such partnership, either in one transaction or in a series of related transactions, which change in composition results in a transfer of capital interest in excess of fifty percent (50%) of the total capital interest within such partnership or results in a transfer of the ownership rights to profit interests in excess of fifty percent (50%) of the total profit interests within such partnership.

SECTION 8. At any time within seven (7) days following the issuance of the certificate of payment of the fee imposed by section 7, the buyer or his legal representative may return said certificate to the trust or its designee for cancellation, together with an affidavit signed under oath or under the pains and penalties of perjury that the transfer, with respect to which such certificate was issued, has not been consummated, and thereupon the fee paid with respect to such transfer shall be forthwith returned to the buyer or his legal representative.

Section 9. The following transfers of real property interests, in addition to those exempt under section 44-25-2 of the general laws, shall be exempt from the fee established by section 7. Except as otherwise provided, the buyer shall have the burden of proof that any transfer is exempt hereunder.

(1) The first seventy-five thousand dollars ($75,000) of the purchase price of the transfer made to a buyer who, or whose spouse at the time of the transfer, has at no time prior to said transfer owned or possessed any real property interest either within or without the town of New Shoreham; provided that the buyer makes the real property interest which is the subject of the transfer the buyer's actual domicile within two (2) years of the time of transfer, and provided further, that in the event of subsequent transfer within five (5) years of the transfer exempted from the fee under this section, other than the transfer of a mortgage to an institutional lender, the fee exempted shall become due, together with accumulated interest and pen-

alties, and in addition to any fee otherwise due as a result of the subsequent transfer. The buyer shall certify and covenant as to the foregoing, and the trust shall attach to the deed a certificate which shall recite the fact that there is running with the land a lien equal to the amount of the fee exempted plus accumulated interest and penalties until such time as all conditions of this section have been met.

(2) Transfers made to a corporation or a partnership at the time of its formation, pursuant to which transfer no gain or loss is recognized under the provisions of section three hundred and fifty-one of the Internal Revenue Code of 1986, as amended, provided, however, that such transfer shall be exempt only in the event that (1) with respect to a corporation, the transferor retains a controlling interest in such corporation after such formation and/or (2) with respect to a partnership, the transferor retains after such formation rights to capital interest in excess of fifty percent (50%) of the capital interest within such partnership or retains rights to profit interest within such partnership in excess of fifty percent (50%) of the total profit interest within such partnership.

(3) Transfers made to a stockholder of a corporation in liquidation of a corporation, and transfers made to a partner of a partnership in dissolution of a partnership; provided, however, such transfers shall be exempt only in the event that (1) with respect to a corporation, the transferee had, prior to the transfer, a controlling

interest in such corporation and/or (2) with respect to a partnership, the transferee had, prior to the transfer, rights to capital interest in excess of fifty percent (50%) of the total capital interest within such partnership or had rights to profit interest within such partnership in excess of fifty percent (50%) of the total profit interest within such partnership.

SECTION 10. A buyer who fails to pay all or any portion of the fee established by section 7 on or before the time when the same is due shall be liable for the following additional payments in addition to said fee.

a. Interest: The buyer shall pay interest on the unpaid amount of the fee to be calculated from the time of transfer at a rate equal to twelve (12) percent per annum.

b. Penalties: Any person who, without fraud or willful intent to defeat or evade a fee imposed by this act, fails to pay all or a portion of the fee within thirty (30) days after the time of transfer, shall pay a penalty equal to five percent (5%) of the outstanding fee as determined by the trust for each month or portion thereof thereafter that the fee is not paid in full; provided, however, that in no event shall the amount of any penalty imposed hereunder exceed twenty five percent (25%) of the unpaid fee due at the time of transfer. Whenever the trust determines that all or a portion of a fee due under this act was unpaid due to fraud with intent to defeat or evade the fee imposed by this act, a penalty equal to the amount of said fee as determined by the trust shall be paid by the buyer in addition to said fee.

SECTION 11 All funds collected by virtue of said fee shall be deposited in a fund to be set up as a revolving or sinking account by the treasurer of the town of New Shoreham. Additional monies or other liquid assets received as voluntary contributions, grants or loans, funds appropriated to the trust by vote of a financial town meeting of the town of New Shoreham, or proceeds from disposal of real property or interests shall be deposited into said account. All expenses lawfully incurred by the trust in carrying out the provisions of this act shall be evidenced by proper vouchers and shall be paid by the treasurer of the town of New Shoreham only upon submission of warrants duly approved by the trust. The treasurer of the town of New Shoreham shall prudently invest available assets of the funds, and all income thereon shall accrue to the fund. Upon termination or dissolution of the trust, the title of all funds and other properties owned by the trust which remain after payment or making provision for payment of all bonds, notes and other obligations of the trust shall vest in the town of New Shoreham

SECTION 12 (a) The town of New Shoreham is hereby empowered, in addition to authority previously granted, to issue bonds from time to time, upon the written request of the trust, under its corporate name and seal for the purpose of financing the activities of the trust under this act. The bonds of each issue may be issued in the form of serial bonds or term bonds or a combination thereof and shall be payable either by maturity of principal in the case of serial bonds or by mandatory serial redemption in the case of term bonds, in annual installments of principal, the first installment to be not later than five (5) years and the last installment not later than thirty (30) years after the date of the bonds. For each issue the amounts payable annually for principal and interest combined either (a) shall be as nearly equal from year to year as is practicable in the opinion of the officers authorized to issue the bonds, or (b) shall be arranged in accordance with a schedule providing for a more rapid amortization of principal, or (c) shall be arranged in annual installments of principal each of which does not exceed any prior installment by more than sixteen (16%) percent of the total principal amount of the issue.

(b) The bonds shall be signed by the town treasurer and by the president of the town council and shall be issued and sold in such amounts as the town council may authorize. The manner of sale, denominations, maturities, interest rates and other terms, conditions and details of any bonds or notes issued under this act may be fixed by the proceedings of the town council authorizing the issue or by separate resolution of the town council or, to the extent provisions for these matters are not so made, they may be fixed by the officers authorized to sign the bonds or notes. The proceeds derived from the sale of the bonds shall be delivered to the treasurer to be deposited in the fund established by section 11 of this act, and such proceeds exclusive of premiums and accrued interest shall be expended (i) for the purchase of real property or interests therein by the trust or (ii) in payment of the principal of or interest on temporary notes issued under subsection (c) or (iii) in repayment of advances under subsection (d). No purchaser of any bonds or notes under this act shall be in any way responsible for the proper application of the proceeds derived from the sale thereof. The proceeds of bonds or notes issued under this act, any applicable federal or state assistance and the other moneys referred to in subsection (e) shall be deemed appropriated for the purposes of this act without further action than that required by this act.

(c) The town council may by resolution authorize the issue from time to time of interest bearing or discounted notes in anticipation of the issue of bonds or in anticipation of the receipt of federal or state aid for the purposes of this act. The amount of original notes issued in anticipation of bonds may not exceed the amount of bonds which may be issued under this act and the amount of original notes issued in anticipation of federal or state aid may not exceed the amount of available federal or state aid as estimated by the treasurer. Temporary notes issued hereunder shall be signed by the treasurer and by the president of the town council and shall be payable within five (5) years from their respective dates, but the principal of and interest on notes issued for a shorter period may be renewed or paid from time to time by the issue of other notes hereunder, provided the period from the date of an original note to the maturity of any note issued to renew or pay the same debt or the interest thereon shall not exceed five (5) years.

(d) Pending any authorization or issue of bonds hereunder or pending or in lieu of any authorization or issue of notes hereunder, the treasurer, with the approval of the town council, may, to the extent that bonds or notes may be issued hereunder, apply funds in the treasury of the town to the purposes specified in subsection (b), such advances to be repaid without interest from the proceeds of bonds or notes subsequently issued or from the proceeds of applicable federal or state assistance or from other available funds.

(e) Any accrued interest received upon the sale of bonds or notes hereunder shall be applied to the payment of the first interest due thereon. Any premiums arising from the sale of bonds or notes hereunder shall, in the discretion of the treasurer, be applied to the cost of preparing, issuing and marketing bonds or notes hereunder to the extent not otherwise provided, to the payment of the cost of the acquisition of real property, to the payment of the principal of or interest on bonds or notes issued hereunder or to any one or more of the foregoing. The cost of preparing, issuing and marketing bonds or notes hereunder may also, in the discretion of the treasurer, be met from bond or note proceeds exclusive of premium and accrued interest or from other moneys available therefor.

(f) All bonds and notes issued under this act and the debts evidenced thereby shall be obligatory on the town in the same manner and to the same extent as other debts lawfully contracted by it and shall be excepted from the operation of section 45-12-2 of the general laws no such obligation shall at any time be included in the debt of the town for the purpose of ascertaining its borrowing capacity. The town shall annually appropriate a sum sufficient to pay the principal and interest coming due within the year on bonds and notes issued hereunder to the extent that moneys therefor are not otherwise provided by the trust. If such sum is not appropriated, it shall nevertheless be added to the annual tax levy. In order to provide such sum in each year and notwithstanding any provision of law to the contrary, all taxable property in the town shall be subject to ad valorem taxation by the town without limitation as to rate or amount.

(g) Any bonds or notes issued under the provisions of this act, if properly executed by officers of the town in office on the date of execution, shall be valid and binding according to their terms notwithstanding that before the delivery thereof and payment therefor any or all of such officers shall for any reason have ceased to hold office.

(h) The town, acting by resolution of the town council is authorized to apply for, contract for any expend any federal or state advances or other grants or assistance which may be available for the purposes of this act, and any such expenditures may be in addition to other moneys provided in this act. To the extent of any inconsistency between any law of this state and any applicable federal law or regulation, the latter shall prevail. Federal and state advances, with interest where applicable, whether contracted for prior to or after the effective date of this act, may be repaid as project costs under subsection (b).

(i) Bonds and notes may be issued under this act without obtaining the approval of any governmental agency or the taking of any proceedings or the happening of any conditions except as specifically required by this act for such issue. In carrying out any project financed in whole or in part under this act, and in the levy and collection of fees or other charges permitted by law on account of any such project, all action shall be taken which is necessary to meet constitutional requirements whether or not such action is otherwise required by statute; but the validity of bonds and notes issued hereunder shall in no way depend upon the validity or occurrence of such action.

(j) Notwithstanding the foregoing provisions of this section, no bonds shall be issued in excess of amounts approved from time to time by vote of a majority of the electors present and voting on the question at an annual or special financial town meeting. A vote not to approve an amount of bonds hereunder shall not preclude any later vote to approve the same or a different amount.

SECTION 13. The trust and all its revenues, income, and real and personal property used by the trust for furtherance of its public purposes, shall be exempt from taxation and from betterments and special assessments, and the trust shall not be required to pay any tax, excise or assessment to the state or any of its political subdivisions.

SECTION 14. Nothing in this act shall affect the eligibility of the town to receive funds under the green acres land acquisition program created under chapter 4 of title 32 of the general laws or under any other state program.

SECTION 15. The provisions of this act are severable, and if any provision hereof shall be held invalid in any circumstances such invalidity shall not affect any other provisions or circumstances. This act shall be construed in all respects so as to meet all constitutional requirements. In carrying out the purposes and provisions of this act, all steps shall be taken which are necessary to meet constitutional requirements whether or not such steps are required by statute

SECTION 16. This section shall take effect upon the passage of this act. The remainder of this act shall take effect upon its approval by a majority of those voting to approve the act at an annual or special financial town meeting of the town of New Shoreham.

ES530

Printed in the USA
CPSIA information can be obtained
at www.ICGtesting.com
CBHW070446030724
11008CB00017B/926

9 781138 050396